TIMOTHY J. McGEE is a member of the Faculty of Music and Scarborough College in the University of Toronto. SHEILA EASTMAN did graduate work in music at the University of British Columbia and is now living and teaching in Toronto.

Barbara Pentland and her music have long been the centre of controversy. As a woman in what many saw as a man's field, her role as composer provoked negative reactions into the 1950s, and her music receives a wide range of responses to this day. Yet even her severest critics acknowledge the highly personal and impassioned quality of her compositions.

This book looks at Pentland's life and career as she moves from her native Winnipeg to study in Montreal, Paris, and New York and at Tanglewood with Aaron Copland, intermittently returning to her home town and gradually becoming known as a performer and composer. The authors discuss various works including *Studies in Line* (1941), which was composed in a highly linear idiom and epitomized her early works; *Sonata for Violin and Piano* (1946), which was based on French-Canadian folk tunes and reflected Copland's abstractness and use of rhythm; and the highly tonal *Symphony No. 2* (1950). Her visit to Europe in 1955 was the catalyst for a profound shift in her work – from the techniques she had adapted from Copland and Hindemith to an elaboration of her own highly distinctive serialist technique.

Since 1958, Pentland's output has been prodigious: fifty works all typified by a marvellously economical use of materials. Some of the most controversial are treatments of the words of modern writers and are inspired by Pentland's passionate concern about contemporary events.

This volume includes a large number of musical examples from her work and photographs of the composer and her colleagues and interpreters.

Pentland giving convocation address at University of Manitoba, May 1976

SHEILA EASTMAN
TIMOTHY J. McGEE

Barbara Pentland

UNIVERSITY OF TORONTO PRESS
Toronto Buffalo London

Toronto Buffalo London
Reprinted in paperback 2017
ISBN 978-0-8020-5562-0 (cloth)
ISBN 978-1-4875-9822-8 (paper)

Canadian Composers / Compositeurs Canadiens 3

Canadian Cataloguing in Publication Data

Eastman, Sheila Jane, 1946–
Barbara Pentland

(Canadian composers, ISSN 0316-1293; no. 2 = Compositeurs canadiens, ISSN 0316-1293; no 2)
Bibliography: p.
Includes index.
ISBN 978-0-8020-5562-0 (bound). – ISBN 978-1 4875-9822-8 (pbk.)

1. Pentland, Barbara, 1912– 2. Women composers – Canada – Biography. I. McGee, Timothy J. (Timothy James), 1936– II. Title. III. Series: Canadian composers; no. 2.

ML410.P25E38 780'.92'4 C82-095125-0

Contents

Preface

There is no need to write a justification for the first extended study of the life and works of Barbara Pentland. For many years she has been considered one of the finest Canadian composers, and the absence of studies of her work – or of that of a number of fine Canadian artists – is to be deplored. There are a number of reasons or excuses for this, which need not be pursued here, but the Canadian Music Centre is taking steps to remedy the situation; this is number 3 in a series of similar studies.

A book about the life and works of a contemporary Canadian composer has different requirements than a similar work on, say, Beethoven, in which a mere reference to a symphony or sonata will immediately bring to the mind of the reader a sound image. The author of such a work can write with the secure feeling that readers will have a strong impression of the composer's style. This is unfortunately not true of composers in Canada today. We wish to discuss Pentland's music for an audience generally unfamiliar with the material (which accounts for the relatively large number of musical examples). This has been a happy chore and we hope you will share with us the pleasure of finding interesting discoveries in each work.

As in the other books in this series, there has been no attempt at encyclopaedic detail of either the life or the music. Those wishing additional biographical detail can consult the master's thesis of Sheila Eastman Loosley, University of British Columbia. There is no source for additional detail concerning the compositions. Following the style of Brian Cherney's *Harry Somers* in this series, representative works have been chosen to illustrate the changes in style and varieties of approach. For a full listing of Pentland's compositions the reader is directed to appendix A.

Perhaps the best description of Pentland's music is the title of her piano tutor: *Music of Now*. Her works are a clear reflection of today. They are vibrant, direct, concise, rhythmic, and vital, truly the music of now.

We wish to express gratitude to the following people who aided us in the writing of this book: to Cliff Eisen, who helped assemble the appendixes; to Harry and Frances Adaskin, Victor Feldbrill, Ron Napier, Godfrey Ridout, Robert Rogers, and Harry Somers, who made themselves available for interviews; to John Beckwith, who provided helpful suggestions, guidance, and much-needed encouragement throughout the project, as he read through the chapters one by one; to the staff of the Canadian Music Centre, especially to Henry Mutsaers, whose cheerful and efficient help with scores, recordings, and copying made the task much easier than it might have been; to Graham Coles, who prepared all the musical examples not in Barbara Pentland's hand; and to Bonnie McGee, who typed the entire manuscript.

Quotations in the text not otherwise identified are from interviews with Barbara Pentland, from her diaries, or from her private correspondence (all quoted with permission). The text of Dorothy Livesay 'Disasters of the Sun,' given on pages 101–4, is from *Collected Poems: The Two Seasons* by Dorothy Livesay and reprinted by permission of McGraw-Hill Ryerson Limited.

This book has been published with the help of a grant from the Canadian Federation for the Humanities, using funds provided by the Social Sciences and Humanities Research Council of Canada, and a grant from the Publications Fund of University of Toronto Press.

S.E.
T.M.
May 1982

ABBREVIATION

CM George Proctor *Canadian Music of the Twentieth Century* Toronto 1980

Barbara and Charles Pentland with their mother, summer 1918

Barbara Pentland, 1923

Margaret Mitchell, Charlotte McConnell, and Pentland, 1933

A light moment

BOTTOM: Copland's class at Tanglewood, 1941; from left: Arnold Chaitman, Sam Morgenstern, Copland, Pentland, Robert Ward, Gardner Read, D.K. Lee

Pentland with Irwin Hoffman,
conductor of Vancouver SO,
November 1953

At UBC, 1950, from left: Gordon Adaskin, Frances Adaskin, Harry Adaskin, John Adaskin, Geoff Waddington, Pentland, unknown

Pentland with three members of the Grunfarb Quartet, Stockholm, 1956

Pentland and her husband in her studio, summer 1981

1

Barbara Pentland in 1982

Barbara Pentland at the age of seventy lives a rather serene life with her husband, John (Hally) Huberman, in a pleasant and comfortable home in Point Grey, Vancouver, near the University of British Columbia campus. She looks much younger than her years, and her calm and confident appearance offers no clue to the avant-garde musical sounds she creates. There are none of the visible signs of intensity that often accompany a serious artist, and nothing that would suggest that her creative life has included a large number of obstacles.

Her bright and attractive studio is devoid of the litter and disarray frequently found in artists' workrooms. She is a very orderly person, and the cupboards and bookshelves that line one wall of the studio contain her library and compositions neatly arranged. Her desk is clear except for the composition she is currently working on – she is always working on one – and the grand piano has only a single gathering of music paper, open to the point where her current work was last interrupted. The walls contain contemporary art works, including an abstract painting by Marion Bembé, a work by Bert Binning, and a print by Paul Klee (on which she based one of her Klee duets in 1958–9). The furnishings have straight modern lines; the cabinets, bookshelves, and desk were designed by her husband.

She is no longer faced with the struggles of learning her craft and the difficulties of seeking a fair hearing for her works. Her life is calm. The days are filled with long hours of composing, interrupted occasionally by letter writing – some of it to university music students in need of help with musical analysis for their current term papers on her music. The yard has a number of bird feeders, and she stops her work from time to time to watch the many birds that light in the trees outside the big windows of her studio or to look at the flowers in the garden (Huberman does most of the gardening). Evenings are spent attending plays, dinner parties, concerts of new music, and occasionally just sitting at home with her husband. Recent vacations, when they both can get away, have consisted of trips to new and exciting places or some snorkelling off the coast of Hawaii or Mexico. She is fascinated by tropical fish and the strange and beautiful new world she has discovered under water. On warm days the two of them go swimming in the ocean at the public beach not far from the house. Outside her studio sits the faithful 1956 Morris Minor that she, and the local garage mechanic, affectionately call 'Eenie-meenie'; and she jokes that the car will probably outlast her!

She can look back on her life of struggle with philosophical amusement. She is internationally respected as a gifted composer and has earned the happiness and sense of achievement that accompany her senior years. Today Barbara Pentland is relaxed. She is a charming and still handsome woman who has weathered, with few visible scars, a lifetime of intermittent poor health, unyielding discouragement from her parents, severe critical condemnation, and a myriad of difficulties all associated with her efforts to become a composer in a man's world. The single-mindedness of purpose required to continue for so many years in the face of so many adversities, where obstacles far outnumbered encouragements, suggests the strength of her character. To live with daily discouragement and more criticism than praise requires enormous self-confidence and a will of iron. Barbara Pentland answers to all of this description, although the composer Harry Somers, for one, sees through a part of her exterior personality:

An interesting characteristic of Barbara as I recall her (and she may never forgive me for making this particular comment), is that very often she would appear as tough as nails, and perhaps even a little crusty to the public and sometimes to her colleagues when she was holding forth on a principle, or an idea, or was under attack. But to anyone who evidenced any real interest or response she melted as fast as the spring snows, and revealed a tremendously warm and responsive person. And this indicated that she really had a pretty strong defensive crust which was very quickly melted with any kind of warmth or enthusiasm.

As Somers discovered, there are two very clear sides to Pentland's personality: a gentle and very charming side, known to her friends, and

5 Barbara Pentland in 1982

an aggressive, unyielding side which reveals itself in her professional life. As a professional she has definite, well-thought-out views, and she learned early in life that the only way to achieve her goals was to hold fast to her positions. But the tough idealist who resigned her position at the University of British Columbia in 1963 over educational goals and standards is the same person who became incensed at the carnage of the Viet Nam war and wept at a play depicting injustice.

If she was plagued with self-doubt anywhere along the way it was never apparent. She has known her goal from childhood and has continued towards that goal regardless of the opposition. She sees herself clearly and seems to be content with who she is; the story of her life suggests that this was always so. She is a very private person who reveals only the most secure elements of her personality.

One aspect of her personality which is occasionally missed or mistaken is an extremely dry sense of humour. Often this is contained in her compositions which, if judged as serious, make little musical sense. She spoofs certain aspects of her own compositional techniques as well as those of other composers. Not all of her humour is dry though, and the more broad aspects can be seen in, for example, the light and folk-like last movement of her *Concerto for Piano and Strings* (1955–6), or in entire whimsical compositions such as *Epigrams and Epitaphs* (1952), which includes an epitaph for herself (see figure).

A story that she tells on herself is a good example of her ability to disguise injury with a wry smile. On several occasions, the Vancouver critic Lloyd Dykk called her music 'arid,' an adjective she found quite annoying. Finally he used the word once too often and she wrote out a piece of music, placed it in an old jar filled with water, and fixed to the jar a label which read, 'Barbara Pentland music, Non-Arid,' and sent it to him. The word 'arid' has not appeared in his reviews of her works since then.

Pentland is interested in current events and is constantly upset by the waves of inhumanity reported in the news. She is especially bothered by the type of matter-of-fact reporting that seems to accept violence and war as a necessary part of civilization. Her composition *News* (1970), a dramatic and bitter satire, records her reaction to the insensitivity of newscasts during the Viet Nam war. She does not speak out frequently on social topics in her music, but her first performed orchestral work, *Lament* (1934), also was a reaction to the sad realities of war.

She has little sympathy for her contemporaries who live in the past with disdain for change. Her own struggles to gain recognition have emphasized to her the plight of women. Her interest in their influences and accomplishments dates back to the days she attended private school in Montreal, from 1927 to 1929. She was struck by the fact that most of the great men in history were reported to have associated with, or married, very well-informed women. When she brought up this information in history class she was told the point was irrelevant; even in a girls' school no one else was interested in the contributions of women in history.

When she later met with constant opposition to her music, seemingly based solely on the grounds that she was a woman, she was still unwilling to accept her 'woman's place' in society and to give up composing. Pentland's fight against accepting her place is a constant theme; it began at home with her parents and continued, virtually uninterrupted, until recent years. She once expressed it this way:

> When I was struggling to be a composer, the fact that I happened to be also a female didn't at first concern me because just to get the education I needed occupied all my attention. About the age of 19 I was signing my compositions using my initials with the surname (and was referred to as 'Mr.' until someone advised me to use my first name), so I must have been aware, but the real impact came later. I was naive enough to believe that if I wrote good music, *that* was what mattered, and I was so absorbed in putting music first in my life I thought others would too. It only came to me *poco a poco* that others thought differently, and the discrimination was very real. It is much more subtle, less obvious than racial discrimination, and therefore more lethal in its effect. I keep hoping that nowadays all this is dying out, and that your generation will be treated more fairly.

The year Pentland spent in Munich, 1956–7, gave an enormous boost to her creative spirit and changed her style of composition, but the equality she had hoped to find in Europe was not present. On one occasion she was introduced to a German composer who was quite cordial until she mentioned that she too was a composer. He immediately turned and walked away. If anything, Germany was even less open to women composers than was North America. That aspect of her trip was a great disappointment.

Throughout her life there have been innumerable stumbling blocks which appear to have been tied to an antagonism towards her sex more than to any other thing. She has maintained a fairly strong sense of identity and purpose through it all, but there is no doubt that the discrimination took its toll. As she reflects on the many incidents today she manages a broad smile and a flippant remark or two, but perhaps her true feelings are revealed in *Disasters of the Sun*. In the text by Dorothy Livesay (Toronto 1976), the Sun (Man) is eventually defeated by the Moon (Woman): 'Sun you are no goodfather but a tyrannical king: I have lived sixty years under your fiery blades.' In setting the poems Pentland deals with the final triumph of Moon not with a fanfare, but with a quiet, tranquil understatement. It is as if woman's triumph was inevitable and not in need of spectacular emphasis. This is Pentland speaking out in her own pointed way. The plot and certainly the musical treatment seem almost autobiographical.

She can look back on a difficult but successful career. For a long time the critics were extremely antagonistic towards the sounds she created, as for example the reaction of critic Hugh Thomson to the première of her *Concerto for Piano and Strings*:

> I've been attending concerts more years than I'd care to count, and last night I had the experience of hearing a work that struck me as quite the most irritating and disagreeable. It was Barbara Pentland's Concerto for Piano and Strings.
>
> The pianist was Mario Bernardi; Victor Feldbrill conducted the CBC string orchestra of 18 players. Place was the network's studio on Parliament St.; the occasion a concert of contemporary Canadian music. It was broadcast across Canada.
>
> I love a piano concerto. The very medium appeals to me – always has. And I have reached a stage where I can listen to the most toe-curling modern work without wincing. But this Pentland opus, I swear, was written with the avowed purpose of exasperating the average listener.
>
> They say to comprehend a new work one should hear it again. Well, if I had to,

I'd take the gas-pipe and end it all. I'm sorry, Miss Pentland, whom I last saw in my own living room some years ago. I like you but could find utterly nothing in your concerto – nor for that matter, in that dreadful radio interview you did from Vancouver before the concert got under way. (*Toronto Star* 13 March 1958)

But even that has subsided: 'The music Pentland weaves through these lyrics [in *Disasters of the Sun*] is in delicate harmony with their disturbing discords of the spirit ... There is a paroxysm of gorgeously vocal, long pliant lines that serve as well to relieve the entire cycle' (Lloyd Dykk *Vancouver Sun* 24 Jan 1977). She no longer has to look for performers who will play her works; for the past decade and a half most of her compositions have been commissioned.

There have been a number of highlights over the years, from recognition at the International Society for Contemporary Music in 1956 to having Pentland Place in Kanata, Ontario, named after her and receiving an honorary doctorate from the University of Manitoba in 1976. She is frequently called upon to represent modern composers in print, on radio, and as a lecturer.

Pentland is highly regarded by her fellow composers both in Canada and abroad, and her compositions are heard with the best modern music all across Canada and throughout the rest of the world. Her style evolved from its roots in the Romantic era to an entirely individual concept of the serial technique and since the late 1960s has included sections of aleatoric (chance) music. She has changed her techniques through the years to fit the changing society she wishes to reflect in her music. And it is precisely this willingness – even eagerness – to adopt new compositional techniques and respond to the changing times that has secured for her a place of importance as a composer in Canada.

During the 1940s, when serious composing in Canada was still a young and unpopulated field, there were only a handful of composers interested in exploring the most modern musical sounds and the latest compositional techniques. Along with Pentland in this risky venture – risky because they surely would not be accepted by colleagues or the average listener – were John Weinzweig and Jean Papineau-Couture (*CM* 33–4). They were willing to adopt the techniques of the more avant-garde composers elsewhere in the Western world and were the first Canadians to venture forth successfully into the turbulent stream of modern composing; their success was Canada's success. Their compositions and those of a few others jolted the country into the modern world of music and were the first evidence of Canada's coming-of-age in the international composing community.

Pentland is a Canadian composer, but she is not a nationalistic composer. One trend in the first half of the century was the use of national subjects or folk tunes as subject matter and raw material for new compositions. This can be seen for example in some of the music by Pentland's teacher Aaron Copland and her colleague John Weinzweig. A few of Pentland's works, such as her opera *The Lake* (1952), exhibit this orientation, and one movement of *Sonata for Violin and Piano* (1946) contains French-Canadian folk songs; but there is little else specifically Canadian about her music. One could better describe her music as representing one of the major twentieth-century techniques in a completely individual style. She takes her place in the community of composers as a part of that rather recent phenomenon, the international modern style that cuts across international boundaries.

2

Early years
1912–1930

Barbara Lally Pentland was born 2 January 1912, the second of three children of Charles Frederick Pentland (1880–1963) and Constance Christine Lally Howell (1883–1961). Charles was a direct descendant of the first 'colon,' Louis Hébert, and the son of a Quebec City lawyer. Charles's grandfather, a Swedish baron, immigrated to Canada in order to escape punishment for his involvement in a duel! Charles grew up in Quebec City, and at the age of seventeen secured a position at the lowest clerical level of a bank. Opportunities for promotion led him first to Toronto and then to Winnipeg where he met Constance Howell and married her in 1908.

In the eighteenth century one ancestor of Barbara's mother was executed for treason by the king of France. More recently, Hector Mansfield Howell, from an impoverished United Empire Loyalist background, married Harriet Lally and moved from Ontario to Manitoba in 1880 as a pioneer lawyer; he eventually became chief justice of Manitoba. As Constance grew up she was made aware of her family's new and exalted social position, a factor that shaped her own life and influenced her attitude towards her own children. When in 1908 she married Charles Pentland, she exchanged a life of comparative luxury for that of the wife of a minor bank official; she never fully adjusted.

In 1912, the year of Barbara's birth, Winnipeg was in the midst of enormous growth. A frontier town, its population had grown from 42,000 in 1901 to 160,000 in 1916, many of the newcomers being among the more than 500,000 European immigrants who came to western Canada. With the immigrants came their household goods, livestock, and special skills. Most people moving west passed through Winnipeg, and many of them stayed. Housing became so limited that new families descended on friends and relatives and sometimes had only one room as a home. Those who settled in Winnipeg, mostly Ukrainian, German, Russian, and Polish, moved into self-contained communities of their own nationality. The city sprawled quickly, with a number of ghettos. It was physically divided by two meandering rivers, three creeks and two major railway lines, the tracks and assembly yards of which further cut up the landscape. These physical boundaries tended to encourage the compartmentalization of the city.

Some of the wilder newcomers enjoyed with abandon the unrestricted gambling and the lax attitude to public drunkenness; the city even had special districts for prostitutes. Both juvenile delinquency and unemployment were severe problems, but at the same time the churches enjoyed unprecedented growth. Many immigrants brought with them a habit of regular church attendance, which resulted in the building of new churches. Soup kitchens in the church basements provided food for the destitute, while increased political pressure from the large new congregations helped create new restrictive laws, for example the Sunday prohibition of milk and bread delivery and streetcar operation.

Barbara grew up in the Anglo-Saxon community, which kept very much to itself; during these boom-town years it had actually become a minority group and, feeling somewhat threatened, developed its own moral codes as protection from the unsophisticated surroundings.

A severe illness in her early youth kept Barbara isolated from more than just the rowdiness of Winnipeg. At the age of four she developed a heart condition which necessitated many hours of lying down and keeping very quiet; as a result, her outdoor activities were curtailed. She had little contact with other children and her mother carefully chose those who would be allowed to visit. There was not much company for her at home: her older brother Charlie (1910–1953) was sent to a boarding school at the age of twelve, and her little sister Christine, eight years her junior, was too young to provide the kind of friendship Barbara needed. Constance tutored Barbara in reading and arithmetic, so well that when Barbara started school at six she was placed with children two years older. This was not wholly an advantage; the older children would not accept her socially and the result was a continued isolation.

Throughout these years Barbara's interest in music was developing. It began as an obvious diversion for an introverted child who spent much of her time alone. She recalls that by the age of six she was sufficiently attracted to music to request piano lessons, but at first her parents refused, probably because of her health. Barbara was not so easily dissuaded and repeated the request frequently over the next several years. Finally, her persistent imploring convinced her parents that she was serious, and when at the age of nine she was to be held back a year in school, piano lessons were granted as compensation.

Her parents never intended music to be anything more than just one of the many cultural activities of a girl in her social class. Constance and Charles had the usual middle-class expectations of a daughter embarking on piano lessons: they wanted a girl who would play pretty pieces for them on Sunday afternoons. But Barbara's interest in piano went further than that and soon she was composing little pieces. Her parents reacted at first with indulgence, hoping no doubt that this interest would soon pass, but as it became evident that she was serious they became alarmed. They expected her to adopt their values and gave her little encouragement or support for her obvious fascination with music. It was at this point that Barbara first became aware of the conflict that would continue to grow in intensity until her mother's death in 1961. As Barbara's plans for her own life developed they came into direct conflict with those of her mother, and neither strong-minded woman ever backed down. There was no single incident that stands out in Barbara's memory as the point where the disagreement began, just an ever-growing awareness that her mother opposed her preoccupation with music.

Constance Pentland had decided on the pattern of her daughter's life even before Barbara was born. She cherished a dream of an elegant and cultured young lady who would succeed in the world of high society; it was probably Constance's unfulfilled dream for herself, which she hoped to achieve through her daughter. It was a way of competing with her own mother and she never reconciled herself to Barbara's refusal to co-operate. Constance's mother had risen to the highest social level in Winnipeg and fully indulged herself in her new position. When Grandmother Howell went shopping she remained in the carriage and a servant fetched the merchants who would come to her for her orders. From the very beginning of her marriage Constance had servants – paid for, no doubt at least partially, with the endowment given to her by her family. Even when Charles was still a bank clerk in the 1910s there was always a cook and a nanny. Barbara recalls that the family went without many comforts during those years and that her wardrobe consisted mainly of hand-me-downs from her Aunt Bessie's family, but servants were a necessity. And at all times Constance lived a life of complete idleness that she believed proper to her social station; it was her lifelong frustration that the final jewel in her social crown, a socially aware daughter, was denied her.

Charles Pentland was constantly torn by the conflict between his wife and oldest daughter. He loved them both but when forced to take sides he could not oppose Constance. Barbara has fond memories of her father; he was a gentle and loving man who did his best for all members of his family. As a child Barbara's vivid imagination often caused her to awaken afraid in the night, and it was always her father who came to comfort her. Throughout Barbara's career he did what he could to help her without antagonizing his wife, but he must have had more than a few hours of discomfort attempting to reconcile the opposing wishes of these two iron-willed women. In at least this one aspect Barbara was her mother's daughter: once she had set her mind on her goal nothing could change her plans. It was left to Charles to steer a course between two strong and opposing currents; neither woman ever changed her mind on the issue of Barbara's goals, and, when pressed, Charles usually supported his wife.

The Pentlands' opposition to Barbara's musical interest grew slowly but without faltering. 'They led me to believe that composition was morally wrong.' At one point Barbara actually did stop composing, but after a few months she felt something lacking in her life; composition provided something she needed, and so she took it up again. 'I persisted because music provided me with an escape into a fantasy world which seemed much more meaningful to me than the real one' (CBC *Thirty-four Biographies of Canadian Composers*, Montreal 1964, 23). The early years of confinement without much social contact and the later rejection by her older classmates encouraged young Barbara to become introspective. Playing the piano and composing provided stimulation and filled her idle hours from an early age and set the pattern for life.

Barbara's schooling began at Rupert's Land College, a private Anglican girls' school. She had advanced so far in her private studies at home with her mother that she was placed at a level equivalent to grade three. Initially, because of her illness, she attended only in the mornings, returning home to rest in the afternoons. She remained at Rupert's Land for nine years but remembers little of the school except the yearly visits of the archbishop; because of his long grey beard the girls imagined that 'he was either God or Santa Claus.'

The teacher chosen for Barbara's first piano lessons was Miss Georgina Lockhart, a young teacher on the school's staff. Barbara began lessons in January 1921 and soon afterwards wrote her first composition:

The Blue Grotto. She recalls writing her first work while sitting in bed one morning, and then having to wait anxiously through the day until she could finally try it out on the school piano – there was no piano at home until later that year when her father bought an old Heintzman upright. *The Blue Grotto* (she does not recall the reason for the title) did not sound quite the way she expected it to, but she proudly presented it to her teacher for approval. Miss Lockhart was not as pleased as Barbara had thought she should be, although she did seem somewhat amused by the efforts of her young student. Barbara recalls vividly, however, that on another occasion soon afterwards Miss Lockhart scolded her for writing a piece in a key she had not yet studied! Barbara continued to compose, but never again showed any of her works to Miss Lockhart.

Barbara wanted very much to be taken seriously and indicated this on the scores of her early attempts at composition; she would secure the signature of her father or mother on each piece in order to prove that she had written it herself. When she was eleven she assembled in a booklet her first five compositions: *The Blue Grotto*, *Twilight*, *Dawn*, *Berceuse*, and *That Darling Old Dad O'Mine*. The manuscript of *Twilight* (see figure) indicates that Barbara composed the work in a single day 'in the down stairs sunroom' of the house in Winnipeg. There is some confusion in the drawing of note stems, and it appears that Barbara has drawn her own crooked staff lines. The first compositions show that she had some understanding of form, melody, and harmony, but there are no obvious indications of the talent she would later demonstrate.

As she progressed through school her piano technique developed and her own compositions often reflected the style of the works she was playing. She acquired the scores of the Beethoven piano sonatas and at the age of twelve attempted to compose a piano sonata of her own. The work, *Revolutionary Sonata*, was never finished although Barbara worked on it for several years (1925–8), continually haunted by the theme and intrigued by the problems of working out a composition in the style of Beethoven. The fragments from it, with their many crossed-out notes, alterations, and additions, show evidence of the long struggle, and its simple harmonies are profuse with scale patterns, turns, appoggiaturas, and trills in an imitation of Beethoven's early style. The piece appears to be in a loose sonata form that Barbara learned by observing Beethoven's sonatas and by consulting articles about composing and musical forms in the *Encyclopaedia Britannica*.

There were no composition lessons during the early years; the only formal musical instruction Barbara received during this period was

TWILIGHT
I
Barbara L. Pentland
PIANO
Page I
By Barbara Lally Pentland, aged 10 years
11 months 26 days. Born at Wellington
Cresent, Winnipeg, Canada on Jan. 2, nd 1912.
(signed)
Page I

piano lessons. She did begin harmony lessons at the age of thirteen, but they soon stopped when it was discovered that she had extremely bad eyesight. Her mother was not altogether pleased with this expansion of her daughter's musical activities anyway, and since the lessons would add additional eye strain, it was a good reason to curtail them. Barbara was determined, however, and armed with a harmony book continued to study on her own. Her private harmony study brought about an unexpected result; it led to the discovery that she had been breaking a number of 'rules' in her compositions. She then tried to adjust her writing according to the rules but was even less satisfied with the series of sterile, stilted works that resulted. Over the next several years (1925–9) she continued to be troubled by the problems of reconciling her creative instincts with the rules that tended to stifle them.

Barbara's reading at that time was limited to the books in her parents' library, which consisted mainly of classic novels. She read a great deal of Dickens and Hugo, though Hugo was removed from her reading list when her parents decided his writing was too morbid. She fed her growing fascination with the French Revolution and for European history in general with historical novels, which at the time she believed to be factual. Her real world, rather severely limited by her parents, was uninteresting, and so she escaped into the world of books, imagination, and music. She was unusually serious for a girl in her early teens; her interests centred around the novels, piano practice, and her growing attraction to composition. Few others her age shared these interests, but by this time she had learned to depend totally on her own inner resources. Her early years of isolation caused by illness had taught her to live without much reference to those outside her immediate family, and her mother's disapproval of her intense interest in music caused her to keep that enthusiasm to herself as much as possible. Her point of reference could be only her own inner drive, which she followed with the singlemindedness she had inherited from her mother.

In Winnipeg in the 1920s there was a constant succession of cultural events, including many performances by touring artists and local groups. In some ways it was a comparatively rich and active place. Robert Turner observed in an article on Pentland:

> Musical interest centered in the amateur choral societies, musical competition festivals, bands and orchestras, as well as on visiting virtuosi of all types; musical standards were mainly in the hands of 'imported English organists' and

choir directors brought over to conduct, adjudicate and train their various groups; and a large proportion of the repertoire was drawn from the choral works of composers such as Handel, Mendelssohn, Parry, Stanford and Elgar. But Winnipeg, at least, was unique in one respect, and that was in having at the doorstep a rich body of folk music indigenous to the French and Slavic groups that had settled in its environs, and, of course, the music of the prairie Indians. (*Canadian Music Journal* II no. 4, 1958, 12)

However, Barbara's secluded life did not allow her to take advantage of the musical life of Winnipeg, and so it was her impression that there was little available in the city. Her musical development had little to do with what was going on in Winnipeg until she returned from Europe in 1930, when, for the first time, she took part in the musical life of the city.

From 1927 to 1929 her education continued at a private boarding-school, the next step in every upper-middle-class girl's education. Miss Edgar's and Miss Cramp's School in Montreal was chosen, probably because Grandmother Pentland lived only a few blocks away. The school provided instruction in subjects as diverse as medieval history, French literature, scripture, elocution, and dancing. The academic side was more than adequate, but the more practical aspects of running a boarding-school were given scant attention. The ladies who ran the school were quite frugal and in the cold winter months the rooms were so icy that even the most hardy constitutions were challenged. Fanatically concerned with illness among the pupils, Miss Edgar and Miss Cramp would isolate any child who was remotely suspected of harbouring germs. In Barbara's case isolation consisted of being sent to her grandmother's to sleep (which delighted them both), and once she was sent home to Winnipeg on the train because of suspected whooping cough.

An unexpected bonus at the school was piano and harmony lessons from Frederick Blair, an organist and choir director, who had been a professor of piano and theory at the McGill Conservatorium of Music from 1904 to 1923. Blair provided Barbara with regular instruction and, just as important, some much-needed encourgement. But even in Montreal she could not escape criticism of her interest in music; she vividly recalls Miss Cramp ordering her to stop playing 'that barbaric noise' (it was a Chopin nocturne!), and the standard punishment for such infractions as reading after curfew was a withdrawal of her piano practice time.

In the spring of 1929 Barbara prepared for the next step in her progression along the path of the proper young lady: she was to embark on a year at the Bertaux finishing school in Paris. It was to be the completion of her education, and her parents hoped she would combine the study of the finer points of being a lady with such subjects as literature, art, and French conversation. Needless to say, they hoped also that exposure to the fine things in life would finally convince their daughter to abandon her ambition for a career in music in favour of an interest in things more fitting a young woman of her station. As Barbara's luck would have it, the experience worked out the other way; it was the first real opportunity to explore to the fullest her interests in piano and composition.

It was decided that the family would take Barbara to Europe, and after registering her at the school in Paris the Pentlands toured England, Scotland, and France, where Barbara's extensive reading of European history served as good background for what she was now seeing. Her diaries are full of details of her impressions of the museums, historical sights, and the countryside:

> At Chichester we stopped at the Cathedral and got out. It is a magnificent edifice because it looks so old and wise and peaceful. The trees are old, the tombstones are old, and such beautiful shady trees, grown throughout the years to be part of the very church, inseparable from it. We walked through the old iron railings, passed many a moldy tombstone and ancient tree to the peaceful quiet of the cloister.

> What a beautiful garden is England – Luxuriant growth such as we have never seen.

> I love the City of London with its narrow lanes and ancient business houses, and splended relics of a city that clung to its freedom and rights through long ages.

On her return to Paris Barbara was invited to accompany Marguerite Bertaux, one of the sisters who ran the school, to Fontainebleau for a few weeks before the beginning of term. There she found the school of music and would linger under the windows listening to the rehearsals and performances within, wishing she could participate. She found a practice room where she could work on her harmony and practice the piano as much as she wished, and for relaxation she roamed the countryside. After the stifling and discouraging limitations she had experienced at home and boarding-school, the freedom in France was truly exhilarating. The Bertaux school was for Barbara the first real opportunity to explore her musical talents and ambitions.

Barbara found the attitudes at the school a welcome contrast to the school in Montreal, 'Fortunately I shall live in a musical atmosphere, unlike Miss Edgar's and Miss Cramp's ... I was thrilled to hear that I am to sleep with a piano.' The two sisters who ran the school were kind and friendly and encouraged a simple, studious atmosphere. Barbara was given three hours daily for piano practice; the school program included, in addition to music, history, French, art history, diction, a well-rounded extra-curricular education including tennis (taught by a Russian count), and frequent trips to art galleries, museums, and concert halls. To some this might have appeared an extremely heavy and serious curriculum. To Barbara it was the fulfilment of her dreams – a school that wanted her to learn all the things she had been struggling to learn for years. It came as a complete surprise when she received permission from her parents to study composition; she was to receive lessons with Cécile Gauthiez, professor of harmony at the Schola Cantorum. Gauthiez had been a pupil of Vincent d'Indy; she was an organist and wrote church music in the style of César Franck. The training Barbara received from her was along the strict lines of the conservatory and included analysis of music by d'Indy, Franck, and Beethoven, harmonization of given melodies, melodic composition in binary and ternary form, cadence formulas, fugues, and motets.

The four-movement *Sonate* (1930) survives from this time and gives evidence that Barbara learned her lessons thoroughly. Each movement has a clear classical form and the melodic shape and Alberti bass figures resemble the early style of Beethoven – her model since her early teens. But the harmonies are far more chromatic than the classic style and demonstrate that she had learned to handle the late nineteenth-century French harmonic vocabulary. (See Example 2.1.) The dedication of *Sonate*, 'A mon cher Professeur Madame Gauthiez hommage respectueux,' indicates the esteem in which Barbara held this teacher who constantly praised and encouraged her with the words 'You have the flame! You must go on!' Barbara had finally found a teacher who recognized her talent and encouraged her to continue. Gauthiez was a thorough task-master and insisted that her student understand the traditional forms and techniques. She was obviously pleased at the way Barbara so thoroughly absorbed the lessons and eagerly went about her work. Gauthiez lavished praise on her and Barbara responded positively to the encouragement and the exercises; both were things she had longed for, and she knew that her time in Paris to enjoy this life would soon end. her diary entries chart her concern with a bit of stylized drama:

7 avril/30 Que c'est triste de penser de partir d'ici. ... 14 juin nous parlons de l'avenir etc. Je commence ma carrière. Elle pense qu'un mari n'interrompt pas une carrière. Elle est la première personne de me comprendre; ce serait difficile de trouver un mari qui le peut. Je vais continuer D.V. de lui prendre des leçons par correspondence. Je l'admire tant ... 8 juillet La certitude que je vais continuer mes leçons avec elle par correspondence m'est un grand reconfort, je ne semblerai pas si loin. Que je l'admire de tout mon cœur. ... 10 juillet Et je pars demain, avec seulement un vague espoir de revenir. O Paris et tout ce que j'aime ici. Madame Gauthiez m'est très chère. Mon cœur fait mal, le sien aussi je crois. Au revoir, et pas adieu – non – ça c'est insupportable.

As the year in Paris drew to a close Barbara became increasingly concerned about continuing along her chosen path. She was learning at a rapid rate but realized that it would not continue when she returned to Winnipeg. She feared being isolated once again from the world of music which she was just beginning to explore. Mme Gauthiez advised her to plan to return to Paris for studies with one of d'Indy's students (she recommended especially Paul Dukas and Albert Roussel), a plan that pleased Barbara. But there was the problem of finances, and so they formulated an additional plan between them: Barbara would attempt to convince her parents to send her to the Eastman School of Music in New York state to study organ. That way she could always support herself with a position as church organist. In the mean time, she could continue her lessons with Gauthiez by mail; it was not ideal, but at least it was a way to continue. It all sounded reasonable enough, and when the year finally came to an end Barbara set sail for Canada in July 1930, with a heavy heart but intent on putting her plan into effect.

3

Musical education 1930–1942

Barbara returned home full of enthusiasm and buoyed up by memories of all her experiences in Paris. For a while she even continued to write her diary in French as a way of savouring the wonderful memories. A few days after returning to Winnipeg her thoughts were still in Paris: 'La Ville est la même, si tranquille après paris! Je suis d'abord très étrange. Ma mère ne comprend pas beaucoup la musique comme je l'apprend, mais je crois qu'elle va aimer que je fasse la composition et l'orgue.' And six weeks later: 'Dans la musique je trouve tous mes amis, mes consolations et mes idéals.' The phrases were a bit melodramatic, but the sentiment was no doubt real.

She would be away from Gauthiez but could still receive guidance by correspondence, which relieved her anxieties about the isolation in Winnipeg. At first the arrangement worked well, and three more works were completed under Gauthiez's supervision: *Trio for Flute, Cello and Piano* (1930), *Aveu fleuri* (1930), and *Sonatine* (1932). But once she was away from the weekly influence of her teacher, Barbara's tastes began to change, and little by little she grew away from the French style taught by Gauthiez – the accompanied melody approach. The lessons-by-correspondence experience was helpful but full of frustrations: a single mail exchange took long months, and several times scores went astray in transit. Finally, when Gauthiez altered the chromatic melody she had written in *Aveu Fleuri* to make it more tonal, Barbara realized that the separation was more than geographical. Gauthiez could no longer guide her along the lines she wanted to pursue; it was time to go her own way and perhaps find another teacher.

At home Barbara was again under the close direction of her parents whose antagonism towards her interest in music was as disheartening as ever. They did buy a new Steinway baby grand for her on her return from Paris, and Barbara hoped it was a sign that they had changed their attitude. It was not so; the piano was an offer to compromise, and Barbara had no intention of compromising her plan to be a composer. She did make some outward effort to please her parents; her diaries mention shopping and attending concerts with her mother, taking badminton lessons, attending the Rupert's Land Alumnae Association meetings and luncheons, and even participating as an officer of the association. But none of this served to disguise sufficiently the basic disagreement. Her parents' ideas of what was best for her continued to dominate the relationship, and a career in music was not in their plans. Instead, a 'coming-out' ball was planned for her eighteenth year, and Barbara was totally dismayed at the thought. She immediately asked that she be allowed to use that money for further music studies, but her parents refused and the ball went on as planned. In their minds her education was finished; they had already spent enough on that aspect of her upbringing and it was time for her to give up all this 'foolishness,' marry, and settle down.

The aim of the ball, of course, was to introduce Barbara to all the 'best' local marriage prospects, and, as Barbara puts it, 'to launch me as a social butterfly.' The tradition was that each young man was to invite her out socially so that she could choose a husband. A rather reluctant butterfly, she turned down the few social invitations that did result. Even in her role as débutante she had only music on her mind. She recalls that 'actually, there was only one interesting person there, an older fellow someone else had brought. He was the only one who knew anything about music.' The ball was as lavish as the Pentlands could afford; both Barbara and her mother wore gowns from Paris. Her diary includes a description of the gown she wore: a model of Blanche LeBouvier, 1830; silk, satin and flowers – just the image her mother had in mind for her. Close to 300 guests were carefully chosen by her parents. 'They invited people they thought I should meet, but I had so little in common with any of them there was nothing to talk about.' Barbara explains that her mother insisted that she look her best, which meant no glasses, and as a result she had a rather blurred view of the whole affair. The ball was an unqualified diasaster which only served to widen the gap between mother and daughter. Barbara felt completely alienated at the ball, and the début had such an adverse effect on her that her diaries, which she always kept when in a positive mood, suddenly cease at that point, not to resume until six years later.

Over the next six years Barbara busied herself in Winnipeg with a number of projects: performing, composing, and learning new instruments. Following Gauthiez's advice to become acquainted with chamber music, she formed a trio with violinist Margaret Mitchell and cellist Charlotte McConnell, which provided her with new repertory and new opportunities to perform. It also stimulated an interest in writing for string instruments and to this end she bought a violin (for $3.50) and secluded herself in the basement to learn how to play it. The experience with the chamber music repertory and the knowledge she gained of the violin served as the basis for a substantial number of compositions she would write in the years to come. Beginning with *Lament* for voice and strings in 1934, her compositions often included string instruments.

The projected organ studies at the Eastman School of Music were not to become a reality. Her parents made it clear that they were not interested in backing more music studies, and Barbara could not afford to live on her own. Instead, she found an organ teacher in Winnipeg, Hugh Bancroft (born 1904), organist and choirmaster at St Matthew's Church. She studied with Bancroft from 1931 to 1933 and was just beginning to feel at home on the instrument when she met Eva Clare, a prominent piano teacher in the city who invited her to be a pupil. Clare was sought out by the best pianists in the area, and the honour of being approached by her caused Barbara eventually to forgo the organ completely in order to devote as much time as possible to piano practice.

After the correspondence lessons with Gauthiez ceased, Barbara continued to compose on her own, although the only source of constructive criticism was the yearly competition of the Manitoba Music Festival. The works she composed between 1932 and 1936 show a development of her skill in handling motifs and melodic material. One of these compositions, *Ruins* (1932), was performed as recently as 1972. It shows a firm grasp of the late nineteenth-century chromatic harmonic practices, and there is far more economy in the use of melodic motifs than in her earlier works. The form she chose is an interesting kind of strophic variation; the text is in three stanzas of blank verse which she set to similar rhythms, but both the melodic curve and the harmony are adjusted to the dramatic needs of the words of each stanza (see Example 3.1).

As 1935 approached, Barbara's relationship with her parents reached an extremely low level. They were unhappy about having an unemployed, unmarried musician around the house, and Barbara was just as unhappy. There were few jobs in those depression days even for the skilled and experienced workers, and Barbara had no marketable skills; the little money she made came from teaching piano. Barbara and her mother were not even on speaking terms for long periods, and she became emotionally depressed and physically run down and finally seriously ill in January 1935. After three weeks of illness she was taken to hospital for a mastoid operation and immediately afterwards caught erysipelas, a highly contagious febrile disease, which resulted in isolation and quarantine. A cerebral thrombosis followed. Recuperation was slow, and although Barbara was able to return home after nearly three months of hospital, further recovery seemed to require a change of scene. She could not recover her strength in the unhappy situation at her parents' home, and they realized that as well. She was sent for three months to Victoria, where the climate and friendly people provided the right atmosphere for recovery of both her health and self-confidence.

Barbara returned to Winnipeg in the fall with new vigour and immediately renewed her lessons with Eva Clare; but it had become obvious that she needed to get away from Winnipeg for further study. Besides the problems at home, Barbara was keenly aware of her need to be exposed to the works of other composers writing in the new idioms and to receive informed critical comment on her compositions. She expressed these thoughts to Eva Clare, who suggested that she send compositions to Vaughan Williams and to the editor of *Musical America*, Walter Cramer. Both men commented favourably on her works; Vaughan Williams suggested further study, and Cramer said 'I find remarkable individuality of expression ... And I think that you should go ahead.' He suggested that she apply to the Juilliard School of Music in New York for further study. She took Cramer's advice and submitted to Juilliard some of her compositions, including *Two Preludes* (1935) and a work she had just finished, *Concert Overture for Symphony Orchestra*, which bears some traces of Vaughan Williams's style. Juilliard accepted her for examination, and an elated Barbara immediately made plans for a 'farewell' recital in Winnipeg.

Throughout the spring and summer of 1936 she prepared for the recital, and in the early fall rented the Crystal Ballroom of the Royal Alexandra Hotel. She engaged a manager to promote the occasion in the hopes that it would provide enough money to pay for her moving expenses – a hope that was not realized. Her program included works by Brahms, Schumann, Shostakovich, Ravel, and Franck and some of her own works, and soprano Agnes Kelsey sang some of her songs, includ-

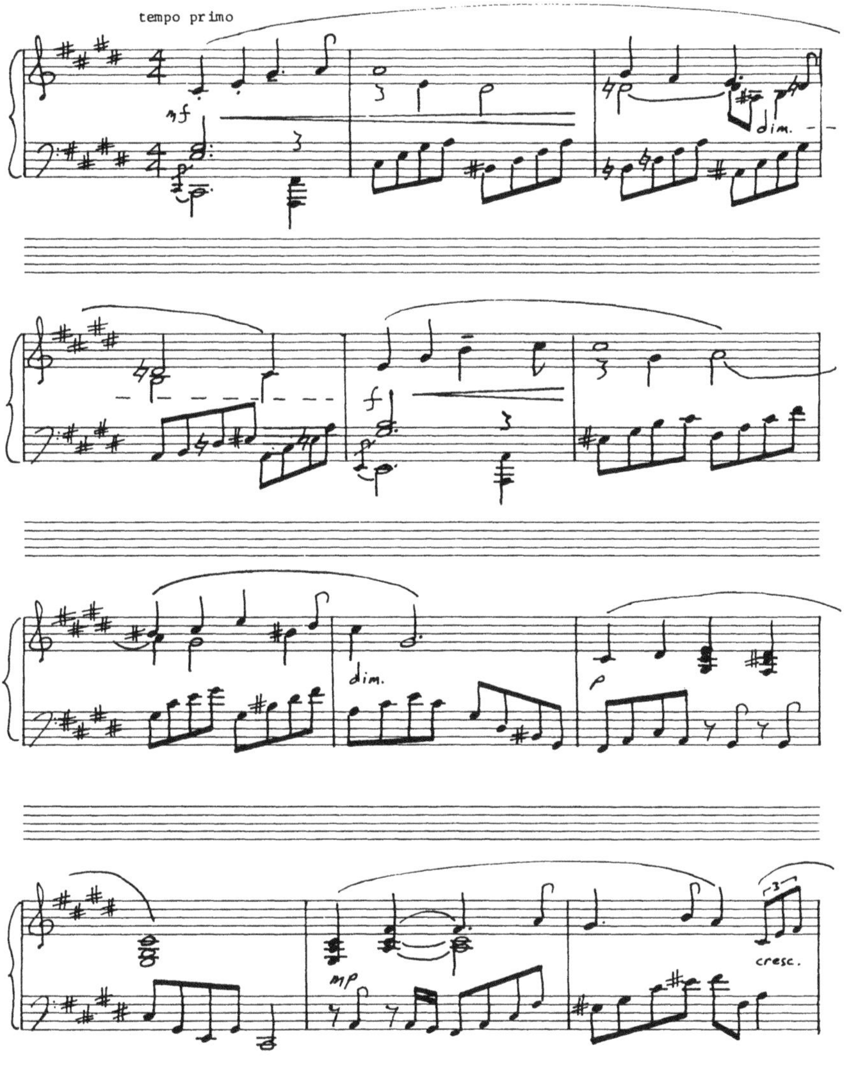

2.1 *Sonate,* 1st movement. See p. 19.

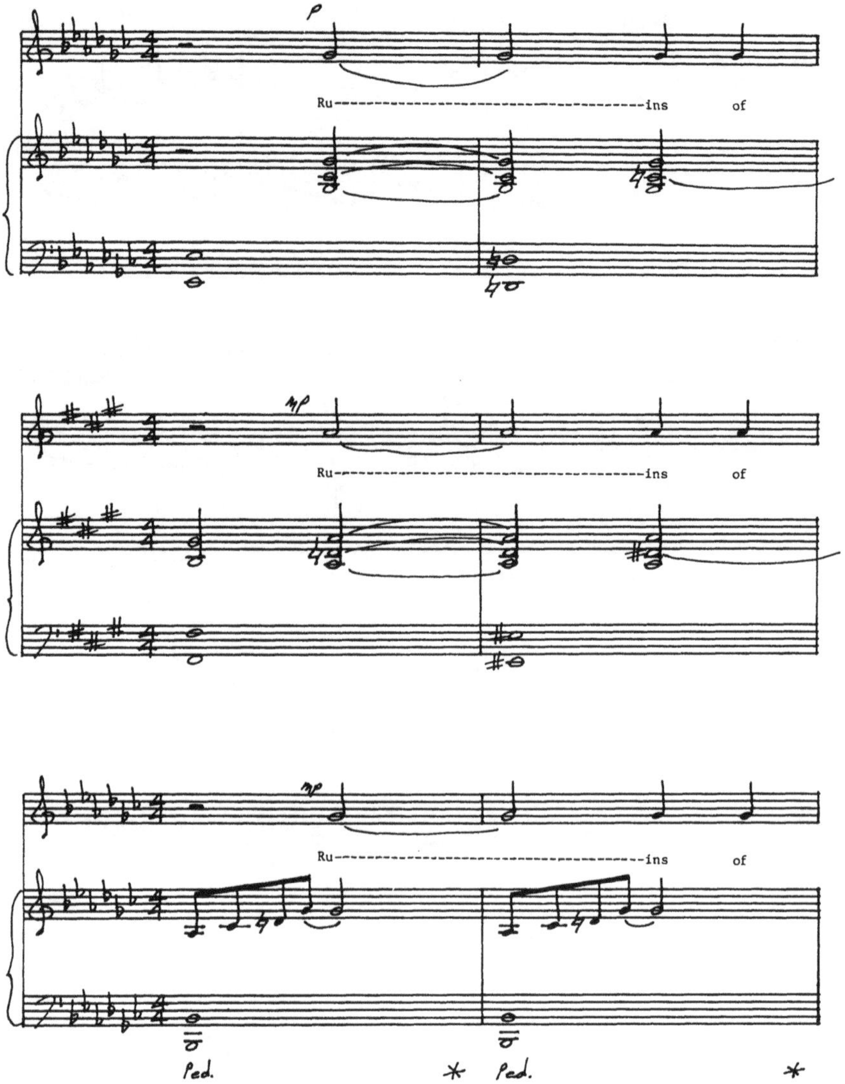
p
Ru------ins of
mp
Ru------ins of
mp
Ru------ins of
Ped. *
Ped. *

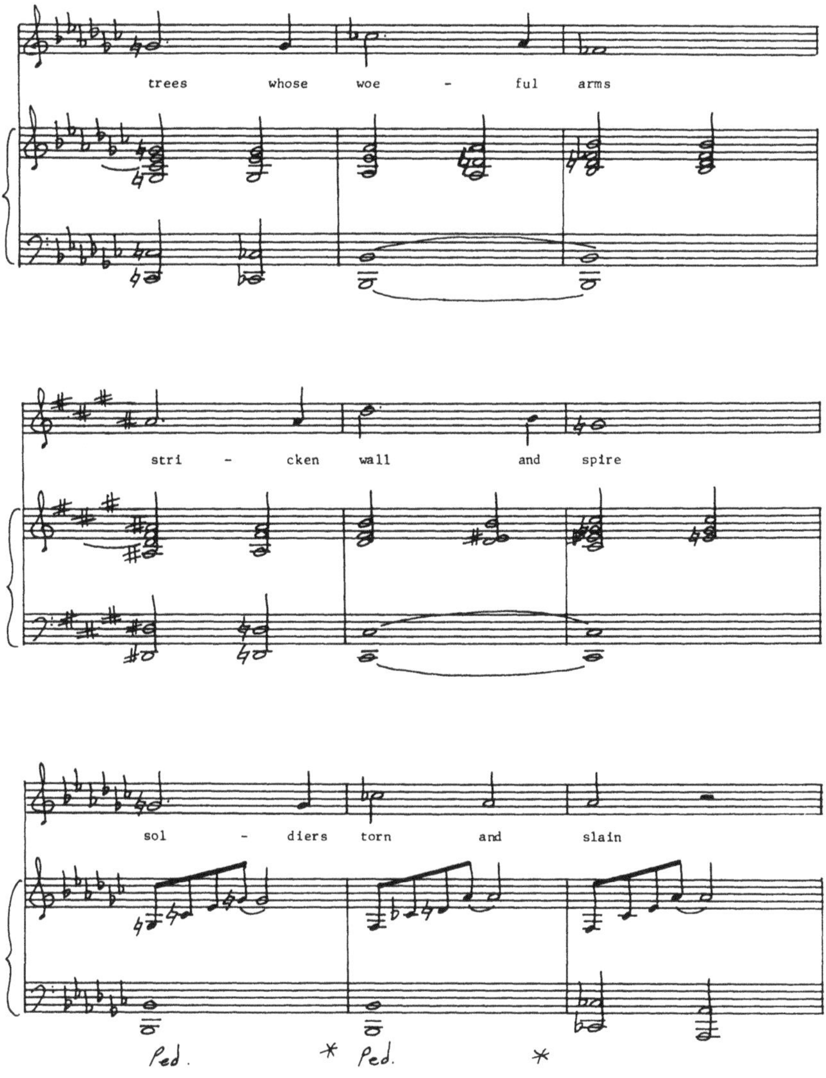

3.1 *Ruins*, bars 10–14, 33–37, 59–63. See p. 23.

3.2 *Five Preludes, Prologue,* bars 1–4. See p. 27.

3.3 *Five Preludes, Romance,* bars 1–3. See p. 27.

ing *Ruins*. The concert was an artistic success and a local reviewer ('A.A.A') lavishly praised both her playing and her compositions, noting that her 'innate musicianliness showed itself' (*Tribune* 22 Sept 1936). The recital was a summing-up of her activities in Winnipeg and a fitting send-off for her move to New York. Her life once again looked hopeful, and her diary resumes at this point.

Upon her arrival in New York she passed the entrance examinations and was awarded a tuition fellowship – a feat she accomplished each of the three years. This also provided her with an opportunity to make an immediate impression on Ernest Hutcheson, president of Juilliard. He invited the new fellowship winners to his Fifth Avenue apartment for a reception and surprised Barbara by asking her to play some of her compositions before the 170 guests. Her technique was still in good form from having just given the Winnipeg recital and she played *Two Preludes* and *Sonata* (1935), which went over very well.

Living conditions in New York were different from anything she had faced in either Montreal or Paris. In place of the pleasant girls' living quarters she enjoyed at the Bertaux school, the choice in New York was limited to a variety of run-down buildings. She rented a room in King's College Club, which was operated by a woman whose several vices included betting on the horses. If she won at the races she would saunter through the dining room saying in a loud voice 'Feed my chickens well!,' but when she lost the boarders shared a less elegant meal.

Barbara struggled along on the money from her father, supplemented by occasional gifts from Aunt Bessie, her father's eldest sister. Bessie (Elizabeth Zoé Pentland Molson), of Montreal, had always been devoted to her brother's family. She was a generous, fun-loving woman, 'a bit stubborn but always with a sparkle in her eye.' She once took Barbara's parents on a European holiday and frequently sent the family gifts of clothing and once even a barrel of oysters! Bessie took a genuine interest in Barbara, encouraging her throughout her career, and often sent money when she thought Barbara was in need. Barbara's life in New York was not lavish, but the financial help she received was enough to help her stay alive and she was far too engrossed in her studies to be aware of the discomforts.

At Juilliard Barbara studied composition with Frederick Jacobi (1891–1952) for the first two of her three years. She best remembers him for introducing her to Renaissance music; she copied out by hand the music of such Renaissance masters as Binchois, Palestrina, Weelkes, Gesualdo, and Lasso and for one assignment made a comparative study of the chromaticism in modal and tonal music. As her study of Renaissance music progressed she became more and more interested in the texture produced by independent lines. This became part of the evolution of her style, which very gradually was changing from a chordal approach to a more linear one.

Although Jacobi expanded her musical horizons, he required Barbara to compose only in traditional harmony. She was eager to please and so she complied, but felt stifled by the limitations. Looking back on the works she wrote while studying with Jacobi, she finds them dull and lifeless in comparison to her earlier works, although the discipline and new techniques provided her with more control and a greater variety of formal organizations. In the first work composed under his supervision, *Academic Allegro* (1937), she conformed to Jacobi's stress on conventional harmony and form, and the result was, in her own judgment, a fairly pedestrian composition with little of her earlier originality. The following year the influence of her study of sixteenth-century modes revealed itself in *Prelude, Chorale and Toccata* for organ; *Leisure*; *A Picture*; *Cradle Song* for a cappella chorus; and *Two Pieces for Strings*. The three choral works were actually contrapuntal exercises written almost completely in Palestrina's style. The orchestral work, which was not a strict exercise, shows some escape from traditional harmony into modality – an interesting combination of the historical technique mixed with the later style demanded by Jacobi. It shows also a great deal of improvement in the handling of string instruments. None of her music from that time actually reflects the interests of Jacobi, however, which included Jewish liturgical music and the music of the Pueblo Indians.

It was the tradition at Juilliard that a student would remain with the same composition teacher for the duration of his studies, but after two years Jacobi decided that, because of her interest in non-traditional harmony, Barbara would be better off with the other composition teacher on staff. Bernard Wagenaar (1894–1971), born in Holland, was a noted violinist, teacher, and composer. His compositional style made use of both polytonality and atonality and his approach to form was neo-classic. This was a better atmosphere for Barbara than Jacobi's stress on the traditional, and even more encouraging was the freedom Wagenaar allowed his pupils. He helped Barbara to develop her own style and to write in a contemporary idiom. He advised his students: 'Take off your musical corsets and write what you feel!' – a view Barbara eagerly accepted.

Living in New York provided an opportunity to hear many concerts, and Barbara's diaries record her introduction to such works as Berg's *Lyric Suite* and Hindemith's *Flute Sonata*, *Kleine Kammermusik*, and *Mathis der Maler*. Hindemith especially impressed her. She played and analysed his piano sonatas and was attracted to his special emphasis on the interval as an independent entity, and on clear horizontal lines. Elements of Hindemith's technique can be found in some of Barbara's works as late as the early 1950s.

The music she composed under Wagenaar's guidance shows a number of different style influences. She was experimenting, in an attempt to find her own style, and although the compositions from that period are all stylistically different, they have in common a vitality and freshness that is undoubtedly the influence of Wagenaar. *Five Preludes* (1938) shows the rather unlikely combination of influences from Mendelssohn, Franck, and Hindemith. Preludes 1 and 4, *Prologue* and *Romance*, adopt the dramatic and lyrical aspects of Mendelssohn's *Songs without Words*. The harmonies, however, have far more chromaticism and dissonance than anything Mendelssohn composed and resemble more the practice of Franck. But the general attitude of the two movements, the kind of melody chosen, and the formal aspects suggest Mendelssohn as a model. (See Examples 3.2 and 3.3.)

Preludes 2 and 3, *Legend* and *Jest*, show a different influence; Pentland used the contrapuntal style, the harmonic ideas, and the rhythmic ideas of Hindemith (see Examples 3.4 and 3.5). In *Legend* the irregular and angular rhythms together with the dissonant counterpoint are reminiscent of the slow movements in Hindemith's *Kleine Kammermusik*, and in *Jest*, the first phrase moves from A sharp in bar 2 to a chord on F, A, B in bar 10 with a hint of Hindemith's tonal freedom and a clear sense of harmonic leading that involves intervallic relationships rather than any sense of chord progression. All the preludes show a rather startling amount of dissonance when compared to compositions of just a few years earlier, as can be seen here for example in the rather dramatic opposition of F and F sharp as the structural notes in the first three bars of *Legend*. The irregular mixture of dissonances and consonances, however, shows that Pentland had not yet arrived at the completely consistent harmonic style that is the mark of her fully mature style; but the basic approach is already present. She was attempting to escape the harmonic and melodic orientation of the Romantic era, and the freedom offered by Hindemith's approach was one of the first steps.

In 1939 the Juilliard School experienced a financial crisis, and the solution adopted was to cut back on the teaching staff and the size of the student body. The teachers who were retained were to have a one-third cut in salary, and all students who had been in attendance three years or more were to be graduated. Barbara had planned to spend a fourth year at the school and was upset at the unexpected curtailment of her studies. In New York she had found guidance, encouragement, and exposure to new music. She had had the feeling of finally finding the right direction for her talents and suddenly it was all to come to an abrupt end.

Her disappointment was given a brief happy interlude in the form of a summer at Edgartown, Massachusetts. Wagenaar invited Barbara and two other students to study with him at his summer home there, and Aunt Bessie provided Barbara with the financial support to make it possible. The setting was just right for work and relaxation. In her diary Barbara described Edgartown as a 'charming unspoiled village of green shutters and shipshape little homes – filled with quiet.' Wagenaar took his students sight-seeing in the area; Edgartown is on the scenic island of Martha's Vineyard in Nantucket Sound. There were many hours spent swimming, lounging on the beach, and in general conversation, and Barbara took advantage of the quiet to finish her *Piano Quartet* and begin work on *Lament* under Wagenaar's guidance.

With her formal study brought to an abrupt halt, return to Winnipeg was unavoidable, and jobs in Canada were fewer than ever. Only ten years had passed since the beginning of the depression, and the country as a whole was suffering. Drought persisted in the prairie provinces, there were hundreds of thousands unemployed, factories were still not in full operation, and export trade was low. In September 1939, Canada began to mobilize its divisions to take part in the Second World War, and within six months the country was fully involved in the war effort. This meant increased government regulation and control, a strict system of quotas, frozen wages, and careful rationing of gas, sugar, and meat.

The general state of political unrest in the world and high unemployment in Canada made returning to Winnipeg difficult for Barbara. She was able to find a few students and shared a teaching studio in downtown Winnipeg with her friend Agnes Kelsey, but this offered only limited financial reward; piano lessons were a luxury that few families could afford. Her only real income, a small one at that, came from her position as theory examiner on the Western Board for the University of Manitoba, a job secured through the kindness of Eva Clare, who was head of music there. Even worse, there had been no improvement in

Barbara's ability to communicate with her mother. The positions of both women had hardened considerably, and Constance refused to recognize Barbara's musical activities as a worthwhile use of her time. Since conditions allowed the Pentlands to afford only one maid at that time, most of the house-cleaning chores were assigned to Barbara – a sign of Constance's utter frustration over her daughter's refusal to fulfil her lifelong dream.

By winter Barbara was in need of a break. By good fortune an opportunity presented itself in January 1940 to take a short trip to Minneapolis, Minnesota. There she met John Verrall, a pianist and composition teacher at Hamline University in St Paul. They had much in common and became good friends. Barbara had heard him perform in a concert in 1929 when they were passengers on the same ship to France, and although they did not meet at that time, she had been impressed enough to keep the program. Verrall took an interest in her compositions and promptly showed her *Lament* to the conductor of the Minneapolis Symphony, Dimitri Mitropoulos, who sent her some suggestions regarding the scoring of the work. Verrall also arranged to have the WPA Orchestra in St Paul read through *Lament* – the first of her orchestral works ever played. The opportunity to hear what she had written, a discussion with the conductor after the reading, and comments from Mitropoulos gave her additional ideas about scoring. The chance meeting with Verrall had broken the spell of gloom and she returned to Winnipeg with more enthusiasm for her work.

During the spring she set about revising the score for *Lament*, and in August the revised version was given its first public performance by the Winnipeg Summer Symphony on a program that included a work by her former organ teacher Hugh Bancroft. The performance was a musical success and succeeded in drawing Pentland's name to the attention of the area's musicians, but she was not prepared for the public reaction. The reviews of the concert were mixed. The critics for the *Winnipeg Tribune* ('S.R.M.') and *Free Press* ('F.A.M.') agreed that Bancroft's composition was beautiful and thoroughly enjoyed by the audience, but their comments (22 Aug) about Pentland's piece were less complementary. The *Tribune* critic said it 'proved very interesting in its modern, colourful harmonies although the abrupt changes destroyed the general mood of the work,' and the *Free Press* critic went a bit further: 'Miss Pentland has strayed from the beaten path. The result is interesting, but one is inclined to think that she has overweighted the piece so that it has the effect of a stunt.' Pentland could accept that kind of uninformed criticism, but she was surprised shortly afterwards to find *Lament* used as the springboard for a controversy carried on in the *Free Press* concerning the role of the artist in society. One listener (C.R. White) felt that artists should stress the hopeful aspects of life (29 Aug).

Chester Duncan came to her defence (8 Sept), stating that artists 'do not make things happen. They merely observe and are honest ... And for the sincere and thereby original success she has had in setting down what she meant ... Her work may well be a landmark in Canadian music.' Although she could not have known it at the time, the controversy and the critics' comments were a harbinger of the reactions her music would cause throughout much of the rest of her career. With *Lament* she had announced herself to the public, and with the newspaper criticisms the public had begun to react.

Pentland's music during the first few years after Juilliard gives evidence of experimentation in a variety of styles. A choral work, *Dirge for a Violet* (1939), uses the sixteenth-century style seen in the earlier choral works; *Unvanquished* (1940), for tenor and piano, is in an extremely chromatic and somewhat dissonant late Romantic style; and *The Devil Dances* (1939) is bi-tonal and somewhat neo-classic. In *Promenade in Mauve* (1940), she shows a bit of her later humour by spoofing her own Mendelssohn-like miniatures. It is a combination of a nineteenth-century melody and twentieth-century dissonances, ending with an unexpected major chord (see Example 3.6). The effect is quite humorous; throughout the composition the rather wayward chromatic melody seems to be doing battle with an accompaniment figure that is in another style and that always contains one note dissonant with the melody. At the end, the melody tires and grinds to a halt while the accompaniment figure triumphantly ends on a bright major chord – but a half-step too high for the melody.

The best features of her early works are combined in *Studies in Line* (1941), which contains a summing-up of the techniques she had been working on since her Juilliard days. The popular works in it have been included on the Royal Conservatory of Music of Toronto piano examination for Grade x. They were published in 1949 (her first published work), choreographed in 1949 for members of the Winnipeg Ballet, recorded four times, and are performed (more frequently in concert than any of her other compositions) by pianists in Canada, the United States, Iceland, Brazil, and various countries of Europe.

Studies in Line presents a good example of Pentland's developing interest in the linear. After it was completed, she realized that each

3.4 *Five Preludes, Legend,* bars 1–6. See p. 27.

3.5 *Five Preludes, Jest,* bars 1–8. See p. 27.

3.6 *Promenade in Mauve*, ending. See p. 30.

3.7 *Studies in Line*, number 2, bars 1–19. See p. 31.

study presented a different kind of line, and so she assigned a title to each in the form of a sketch which describes the type of contour within the piece (left to right numbers 1–4):

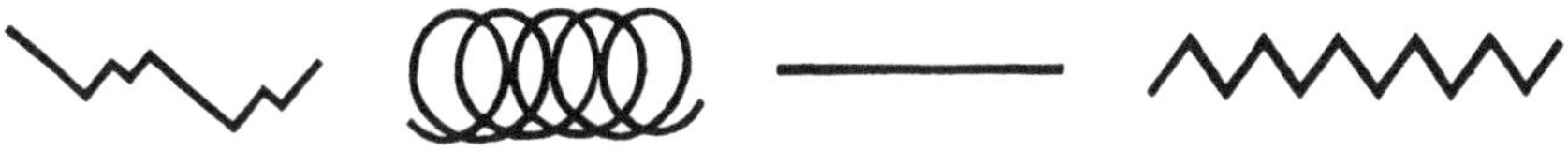

She brings to these works a skill with several different techniques: counterpoint (numbers 2 and 4), a bit of neo-classic lyricism (numbers 2 and 3), nineteenth-century drama (number 1), and a taste for dissonance in all of them that is the result of the bi-tonality of two separately oriented parts. Number 2 is a good example of her summary style from this period.

The interlocking circles of the title clearly express the linear orientation of number 2. The overall form is a miniature rondo, and the character is that of a seventeenth-century *giga*. The principal theme is a canon. The lower part chases the upper, and the two lines weave in and out of one another in a circular motion until the contrasting second theme abruptly stops the forward motion (see Example 3.7). Although the melodic material is much the same for both parts, in general they trace separate tonal patterns which, in the opening bars, suggest vaguely the simultaneous keys of G minor and B minor. But after the first measure the listener hears the two lines at once and the separate tonalities are not obvious. What is heard is a very restless motion that constantly reorients itself as first one line moves and then the other. The overall impression of tonal orientation is D – both D major, as in the triads formed in bars 3, 4, 6, etc, and D minor, in later measures. The harmonies resulting from the combined tonalities of the lines are sometimes consonant and sometimes dissonant, but without any discernible pattern. The melodic pattern begun in bar 1 is repeated in bar 2 by the second voice with the same intervals but beginning a sixth lower. This concept of imitating intervals rather than specific notes is a technique as old as the Renaissance and has been in constant use since that time. In this work we see it adapted for use in bi-tonality. The concept was destined to become a major part of Pentland's later style.

Pentland demonstrates in this set of pieces a clear command of her craft. Each of the studies contains a single distinct mood and contrasts with all the others, and yet each one bears her particular kind of directness of line and handling of dissonance. *Studies* is her first composition that bears the individual mark of the composer, rather than being a combination of influences. Pentland has synthesized the various styles and techniques she had studied and experimented with and has produced a composition in a style uniquely her own.

She entered *Studies* in the Wednesday Morning Music Club competition in Toronto, but by this time she was wary of making competition judges aware that the composer was a woman, and so she submitted the work under the name Ernest N. Devor, a name she had used before in such circumstances. The adjudicator, Dr H.A. Fricker, noted that the composer 'has an original mind for musical composition and logical development in his thoughts,' but obviously had little appreciation for modern sounds. Along with the praise he also remarked that 'the music is evidently not designed to give pleasure.'

The clarity, directness, and relative simplicity of *Studies in Line* place it among Pentland's most accessible works. She must have thought this when she decided to play it during an interview in the early 1940s. The University of Minnesota was looking for a 'composer-in-residence' and Pentland applied. The interview seemed to be going well, and when finally she was asked to play one of her works, she confidently chose what she thought was her best: *Studies in Line*. She had obviously misjudged the committee; when she finished playing they sat still with looks of shock on their faces. No one knew what to say until finally, after a long and ominous silence, one of them intoned, 'When you came in I thought you were a *nice* girl.' She did not get the position.

In 1940 and 1941, Pentland was presented with three opportunities to write dramatic works. The first of these was a radio drama entitled *Payload*, a story of the development of the Canadian north through aviation. The script-writer, Margaret Kennedy, had commissioned poems by the Canadian poet Anne Marriott for dramatic presentation and needed a musical score to support the strong images. The Marriott poems describe the landscape as 'bare ice, hard grey rocks watching with venomous eyes ... The strange land grins and chuckles to itself.'

Program music was new to Pentland and she consulted with Marriott, who visited her in Winnipeg to discuss the moods involved. To match the images, Pentland orchestrated the score for winds, percussion, and piano, which helped her portray the strong, barren scenes described in Marriott's poetry. Pentland was so absorbed by the assignment that she completed the score of seventy-four pages in three days! *Payload* was performed on CBC radio in Montreal and was described in the *CBC Programme Schedule* (31 Jan 1943) as 'one of the sensational radio successes of 1940.' Soon afterwards it was heard through the British

Broadcasting Corporation (BBC) in London and the Australian Broadcasting Corporation (ABC) in Sydney. The BBC broadcast was arranged by the Quebec Musical Competition Festival officers, who were sufficiently impressed by the drama to propose to the BBC that it consider broadcasting the Canadian radio recording. The letter from Quebec arrived in London shortly before the BBC office was hit by a bomb, and four months later an embarrassed BBC officer replied to the letter explaining the delay and relating the information that the BBC liked the drama and intended to broadcast it soon.

Another collaboration with Mariott did not meet with such success. Pentland was asked to write the music for a radio drama based on Marriott's book *The Wind Our Enemy*. But when the score was completed in early 1941 the entire work was rejected by the CBC. Pentland feels that it was because of the intensity of the drama: 'They wanted more cheery entertainment for the country during the war years.' Whatever the reason, the drama was never broadcast.

A different and more successful project was *Beauty and the Beast*, a children's ballet-pantomine for two pianos, commissioned by Gweneth Lloyd for the Winnipeg Ballet Club (later the Royal Winnipeg Ballet). The work was choreographed by Lloyd and performed in January 1941, with the composer at one of the keyboards.

While Pentland was enjoying increased recognition in Winnipeg, her efforts to find steady employment continued to meet with little success. She contacted several teacher-placement agencies in the United States, but there were few positions open, as all of North America was involved with financing a war. An influx of refugees from Europe reduced the possibilities for employment outside music, and Pentland found herself still living at home, a handful of piano and theory students her sole source of income.

The commissions had reassured and encouraged Pentland. She was grateful for the self-confidence they gave her. She had continued to develop along the lines she had learned in New York and longed for that type of exposure and competition. Although full-time study was not possible, she decided to apply for the 1941 summer course at the Tanglewood Music Festival in Massachusetts, the summer home of the Boston Symphony. This summer festival had begun in 1934, and in 1940 The Berkshire Center was established to offer summer courses for young people to study with established musicians and to participate in performing groups. It was an immediate success and attracted a large number of fine young performers and composers.

Pentland submitted *Beauty and the Beast* and two movements from *Little Symphony for Full Orchestra* (later retitled *Arioso and Rondo*) and was selected as one of the six to study composition with Aaron Copland. She could not have hoped for a better opportunity to measure herself against other young composers. Also studying at the centre that summer were Lukas Foss and Leonard Bernstein. Pentland also attended a survey course in medieval and Renaissance repertory, taught by Paul Hindemith, and sang in a chorus of composition students under his direction. Hindemith's tastes in music encompassed everything from the middle ages forward and he felt strongly about exposing the young composers to a wide variety of styles. The chorus repertory included music from the twelfth century to the latest works composed by the students themselves. As the only female in the chorus, Pentland sang tenor.

The opportunities for exposure to a wide range of music seemed endless. The practice rooms echoed with the sounds of all kinds of instruments. A variety of student ensemble rehearsals and performances went on all day; and the Boston Symphony played in the evenings. The composition students were allowed to attend orchestra rehearsals, and the principal players from each section of the orchestra visited composition class to demonstrate the technical capacities of their instruments, to answer questions about their instruments, and to try out passages written by the students. This was especially important to Pentland since she had not had much exposure to some of the wind instruments. The summer of 1941 was so productive that she returned for an equally rewarding session the next year.

The private composition lessons with Copland proved to be a great help for Pentland. Like Wagenaar, he did not encourage his pupils to emulate his style but instead urged them to develop a style of their own. One of his comments on Pentland's compositions was that they showed Hindemith's influence in their heaviness, and he suggested she lighten her style. He also suggested that she work more carefully within specific traditional forms in order to more tightly unify her works. Most of all, he told her she had studied enough *about* composition; the next step was simply to write and find her own style.

Pentland was impressed with both Copland and his compositions, and it was probably unavoidable that she would pick up some elements of his writing style. She was attracted by his facility with rhythms and classical forms, but did not realize at the time how much she was influenced. When looking back on her works, however, she realizes now

3.8 Aaron Copland, *Piano Variations* (copyright Boosey & Hawkes 1956). See p. 35.

3.9 Barbara Pentland, *Variations for Piano*, bars 1–12. See p. 35.

Allegro risoluto ♩ = 132-152
mf
sul III
p
tranquillo
p
sf
sf

3.10 *Sonata for Violin and Piano*, 3rd movement, bars 1–8; bars 47–53; bars 107–14. See pp. 35–6.

3.11 *Sonata for Violin and Piano*, 3rd movement, bars 178–184. See p. 36.

how much of Copland is present in the first of the three short piano pieces, *From Long Ago* (1946), and especially in *The Living Gallery*, a 1947 film score. Copland's film music was well known in the 1940s. The films he scored, *Of Mice and Men*, *Our Town*, *North Star*, *The Red Pony*, and *The Heiress* (for which he won an Academy Award), were popular in Canada. When Pentland was commissioned by the National Film Board to write for *The Living Gallery* she unconsciously modelled her score on the Copland works. The lightly scored, rhythmic, and 'folksy' melodies all bear a close likeness to those of her teacher, but it was not until she heard the score many years later that she realized how uncomfortably close it is to Copland's writing. She had intentionally used his approach, but had believed she had successfully adapted it to her own style.

Even Copland's earlier, more abstract style had some effect on Pentland. *Variations for Piano* (January 1942), her first composition written between the two summers at Tanglewood, bears a remarkable resemblance to Copland's *Piano Variations* (1930). In Examples 3.8 and 3.9 the themes of the two sets of variations clearly demonstrate the superficial similarity of the two works. Both works use an accented up beat as the initial motive; the texture of both themes is spare; and both themes are composed of short motifs. The treatment selected for some of the variations also shows that Pentland knew the Copland work and was attempting to learn his approach by writing a work with an attitude similar to his.

Of the various characteristics of style she learned from Copland, the one that obviously impressed her most was his use of rhythm. Copland had a way of selecting a short, memorable, dance-like rhythm as a principle motif for a work, and Pentland has frequently returned to this device, when a light sounding movement is required, as can be seen in her selection of rhythmic motifs for the third movement of her *Concerto for Piano and Strings* (1955–6) and the entire third movement of *Sonata for Violin and Piano* (1946) (Example 3.10, below). The third movement of *Sonata* draws on folk tunes for its basic melodic material, a source used by Copland in his compositions from the mid-1930s to the late 1940s.

For the third movement Pentland chose three French-Canadian folk tunes, 'Je le mène bien mon devidoi,' 'J'ai perdu mon amant,' and 'Mon père a fait bâtir maison,' which she put together in a form similar to a rondo (or a 'Folk Rondo' as she calls it in the score). Each tune is introduced and expanded separately; the individual motifs of each are developed and recombined; and then tunes one and three are brought back before a final coda. The three tunes have contrasting characters and in combination they make a light and charming finale for the sonata. In the initial statements of the folk tunes the melodies are presented intact, and for accompaniment Pentland selected two devices often used by Copland: open fifths and tone clusters. During the opening bars of the first tune the accompaniment is based on motion in parallel fifths; for the second tune the accompaniment is tone clusters, and for the third, fifths in contrary motion. (See Example 3.10.) Once the three tunes have been introduced with their accompaniments, Pentland develops them by combining the melodic and rhythmic motifs, and also by exchanging and mixing the accompaniment patterns, as for example in Example 3.11, where melodic motives from tunes 1 and 3 are accompanied in the style of tune 2. The folk tunes in this movement are Canadian and the style of writing is definitely that of Pentland – especially her use of dissonance; but the approach and rhythmic vitality can be traced to the influence of Copland.

The lessons with Copland and classes with Hindemith had provided her with an exposure to a variety of compositional ideas and the confidence to continue to develop her own style. There is no point in her career when she has stopped learning or incorporating new ideas into her compositions, but at the close of the Tanglewood session of 1942 she accepted Copland's advice to go off on her own. This marks the end of her formal training and the beginning of the first stage of her mature writing.

4

Early style 1941–1948

Toronto seemed to be the key to the next step in Pentland's career. She had stopped off there in 1941 for a few days on her way home from the first summer at Tanglewood and met several composers and performers, among them Harry Adaskin, Godfrey Ridout, and John Weinzweig. They all had much in common, and her new friends, especially Adaskin, encouraged her to move to Toronto. Little was going on for her in Winnipeg, and she could see that in Toronto she would benefit in many ways. A number of her compositions had already been performed there in concerts arranged by Adaskin: *Piano Quartet* in May 1941, and, even earlier, *Five Preludes* and *Rhapsody 1939* were played at a Junior Vogt Society concert. If she was to develop as a composer she needed constant exposure to new ideas and an opportunity to hear her works performed regularly, and in Canada that meant that she had to be in Toronto. Following her second summer at Tanglewood, in 1942, she moved to Toronto.

Toronto was developing the types of opportunity a composer needed. It had a symphony orchestra that was improving rapidly, a number of chamber ensembles that played frequently, many fine soloists eager to perform, the largest of the CBC broadcasting facilities, the most prominent conservatory in Canada, and a relatively large, sophisticated population. This is not to say that modern music played a big part in Toronto in the early 1940s. The conductor of the Toronto Symphony, Sir Ernest MacMillan, was not overly enthusiastic about the newer trends in composition, although he sampled some of it. His audience was unsympathetic towards most of the music of the twentieth century, but he patiently attempted to educate it and broaden its tastes without arousing its ire in the process.

The symphony featured the usual repertoire of Bach, Beethoven, and Brahms, but works by contemporary Canadians and English composers – although not the most avant-garde – were regularly interspersed in the program, and the audience frequently saw Canadian soloists such as Zara Nelsova, the principal cellist with the orchestra. The war effort encouraged a spirit of nationalism which affected many aspects of Canadian life and also stimulated interest in Canadian music. Audiences were larger, there were more performances, and the press gave better coverage in both quantity and quality. Canadian composers whose works were performed by the Toronto Symphony during the early 1940s included Robert Fleming, Alexander Brott, and the Torontonians Ridout and Arnold Walter. Still, even in 1946 MacMillan felt the need to request a 'spirit of tolerance' from his audience before conducting a performance of Sibelius's *Symphony No. 4* (1911) (*CM* 33). The most noted Toronto composer at that time was Healey Willan, whose music and sympathies were definitely not with the more modern sounds. But there was more potential in Toronto than in any other Canadian city, and Pentland joined the small group of 'pioneers' who were to be major influences on the development of both the compositional techniques and the broadening of musical tastes in Canada.

Violinist Harry Adaskin was very active in the field of modern music. Together with his wife, pianist Frances Marr, he performed a wide variety of music, including new works by young Canadian composers. The Adaskins were very friendly and helpful to Pentland; they obviously were attracted to her music and performed it on numerous occasions during the 1940s and 1950s. In 1945, Adaskin told a Winnipeg *Tribune* critic that he considered Pentland to be one of the three or four great musical talents in Canada. 'I consider Barbara Pentland a first-rate talent, as good as Russia's Shostakovich or Aaron Copland and Roy Harris of the U.S.'

Godfrey Ridout had been composing and teaching in Toronto with some success since 1939. He and Pentland became good friends immediately, and he speaks of her with admiration and affection. 'We all could see right from the beginning that she was something special; all you had to do was hear *Studies in Line* and you knew.' He suspects that one of the reasons the friendship lasted was because he and Pentland offered no threat to one another. They composed in quite different styles and so could always be mutually supportive without feeling any spirit of competition. His admiration for her work has never wavered, although Pentland had little time for his less avant-garde style. He recalls that she once left in the middle of the Toronto Symphony performance of his *Two Etudes*, muttering to no one in particular 'nineteenth century'! But Ridout could pass off this incident knowing Pentland's single-minded commitment to her own pursuit of the more modern sounds. He remembers that she was quite popular with the small group of performers and composers. 'She was always good company – lots of fun, and she had an excellent knowledge of a rather wide repertory.' After concerts, he recalls, she would often throw impromptu parties in her apartment in an old coach-house and they would all sit around and discuss music.

Pentland's friendship with Weinzweig was not as constant as that with Adaskin and Ridout. His music was similar enough to hers that a sense of competition was often present in their relationship, and while they shared a degree of comradeship there was always a feeling of rivalry lurking beneath the surface. Weinzweig has been the most influential composer in Canada since 1950, and his growing importance was apparent in the 1940s. As early as 1939 he had adopted elements of the serial technique in his compositions which marked him as the most avant-garde composer in Toronto. The serial (or twelve-tone) technique, which was developed by Arnold Schoenberg and his circle in the 1910s, uses all twelve tones of the chromatic scale equally. A number of variations and approaches were developed within the broad outlines of the technique, but all result in dissonance in a quantity not accepted by the general public in 1940. Weinzweig's prominence resulted from the high quality of his compositions, his influence as the teacher of the most active Canadian composers in the third quarter of the century, and his position as outspoken leader of modern music in Canada. He has continually championed the cause of contemporary compositions and composers. When Pentland first met Weinzweig in 1941 he was especially happy to find a kindred spirit. He was tiring of his role as the 'wild radical' at the Toronto conservatory, and welcomed another composer who was experimenting with new techniques. They found much to discuss during that first visit, and after Pentland returned to Winnipeg, Weinzweig's letters kept her informed about musical happenings in Toronto.

From Weinzweig she heard that her composition *Studies in Line* was selected, along with works by Louis Applebaum, Hector Gratton, André Mathieu, Ridout, and Weinzweig, for a special presentation of Canadian music in New York during January 1942, at a concert sponsored by the US League of Composers. The concert was the first all-Canadian concert given in New York and was considered an important musical event. Canada's assistant trade commissioner, James P. Manion, opened the concert with an address and read a telegram of good wishes from Prime Minister Mackenzie King. The critic for *Musical America* made favourable remarks about all the compositions and singled out the works of Weinzweig and Pentland for special comment. He said that they 'reveal unmistakably the impregnation of the more extreme modernistic school' (25 Jan. 1942). To Pentland and Weinzweig this was praise, no matter how it was intended.

The first year in Toronto was rather difficult. Once again she was financed by her father, with some help from Aunt Bessie, but she was constantly short of money. Because of the war it was difficult to find students, and so she took a job in a small crafts workshop for 25 cents per hour. She set up a small teaching studio in the second-floor flat of a cold, old house and, as an economy measure, lived in the same quarters, but caught pneumonia, which interfered with the little teaching she did have.

The following year she joined the staff of the Toronto Conservatory of Music to teach theory and composition, and her fortunes began to improve. At first she shared a studio with Weinzweig because the conservatory position provided only a few more pupils than she had on her own. But when the war ended, and returning servicemen were given government subsidies, teaching turned out to be a more substantial source of income. She has very pleasant memories of teaching the servicemen; they added new life to the program at the conservatory. They were happy to have such an opportunity and were dedicated workers. Some turned out to be the best pupils she ever had, although none ever pursued composition as a career.

Pentland's other source of income, at the University Settlement Music School, sparked an interest in teaching young people that has continued to inspire her. An invitation came to teach creative music to underprivileged children aged five to eight, and she accepted it as a challenge. For three years she encouraged the children to write their own songs and to respond freely to everything around them. The closing program of each session included each child conducting his own song while the rest of the class sang. The children enjoyed the experience and were quite inventive. For Pentland the experience produced insights and ideas for the creative series of piano works she turned out in later years.

In spite of the initial hardships, it was obvious to Pentland that she had made a wise choice in moving to Toronto. She was at the hub of Canadian musical activity and could take advantage of numerous opportunities to forward her career. Her works were performed regularly in concerts; a sampling of the performances during the 1940s gives an indication of that success. Her *Piano Quartet* was first presented in Toronto in 1941 on a Junior Vogt Society program, and was performed by the Society for Contemporary Music in 1943 and at the Art Gallery in 1944. *Studies in Line* was presented in Toronto at least once a year (and frequently elsewhere in the world). Harry Adaskin played the première performance of *Concerto for Violin and Small Orchestra* (1942) in Toronto in 1945 and played it several times afterward (including a New York recital in 1948). In 1948 Harry Somers presented an entire recital of her piano works, which included compositions from 1938 to 1947.

Pentland and her music also appeared with increasing regularity on CBC radio in performance and interview. An extended series called 'Our Canada' was aired in 1942 and 1943, originally with the intention of telling Canadians all about their country. One of the last programs, 'The Arts Grow up,' generated such interest in Canadian music that an epilogue devoted solely to composition followed. Entitled 'Music for Radio,' it consisted of music written especially for radio and included Pentland's *Payload* and music by Howard Cable, Ridout, and Weinzweig. An outgrowth of this was a program in February 1943 consisting entirely of Pentland's music and an interview with her. There was another CBC radio commission in 1944, *Air-Bridge to Asia*, for a program commemorating the second anniversary of the opening of the Alaska highway. In 1946 another series on Canadian composers, broadcast throughout Europe as well as Canada, included three of Pentland's compositions.

Pentland's international reputation continued to grow through the decade. In 1948 her *Cities* from *Song Cycle* (1942–5) was awarded a bronze medal at the Olympic Games in London; the following year she was the only Canadian selected for a special concert in Philadelphia entitled 'Chamber Music by Women of Five Countries' at which her *String Quartet No. 1* had its première. Shortly afterwards *Holiday Suite* (1941) was presented by the World Festival of Youth and Students in Budapest in an all-Canadian concert given under the auspices of the World Federation of Democratic Youth.

In the music written between 1941 and 1948, beginning with *Studies in Line*, Pentland settled into what might be called her 'early mature style,' that is, compositions written after the more eclectic student days and in a style more individually her own, but before she adopted the twelve-tone ideas. The advice given by Copland, to write within established forms, had been taken seriously, and most of the works written during these years fall into fairly easily identifiable standard forms. The sounds within these forms, however – the harmonies, melodies, and textures – present a very modern and very personal style. For the first time there are enough individual characteristics and consistent approaches to identify a 'Pentland' style that stands apart from the works of her teachers and models. There is a unity of technique within the variety of the music that tells us Pentland has identified herself; she has found her own way of communicating through music.

Her values and objectives are expressed in an article she wrote in the *Canadian Review of Music and Art* in 1943. 'On Experiment in Music' attempts to give some historical perspective to the musical experimentation of the twentieth century. Pentland draws on her knowledge of compositional changes from the seventeenth century forward to justify her point that experimentation is 'the sign of vitality in art, the will to live, which becomes particularly active following a period of great production in which all existing means seem to have been exhausted ... Perfection brings revolution.' We can extract her values from her description of the changes in the twentieth century and from her selection of examples: Erik Satie is singled out for praise because he simplified musical expression. In comparison to the late Romantics 'he took music down from the exalted pedestal it had achieved and guided it toward a fresher atmosphere by stripping it of all pretentiousness.' Schoenberg and his followers are described as having developed a 'highly emotionalized feeling,' but Pentland stops short of praising the serial technique. Instead, Hindemith is pointed out as following a 'newer direction' in which he 'treats music as art and not as an emotional outlet,' and she quotes Copland's evaluation of Stravinsky's early works as 'a rhythmic hypodermic.'

Her praise for the simple approach of Satie, the non-emotional music of Hindemith, and the rhythmic vitality of Stravinsky is in reality a description of her own objectives at that time. The music she was writing in the early 1940s contains all of these elements, and even in the subsequent changes of technique in later years these elements continue to be present. At first it would seem that the most obvious change of mind was in reference to the music of Schoenberg when, in 1955, she adopted the serial technique. But even in this matter she was consistent. What she found objectionable in Schoenberg's music was the emotionalism, and when she finally used the serial technique it was after she had

4.1 *String Quartet No. 1*, 1st movement, bars 1–10. See p. 43.

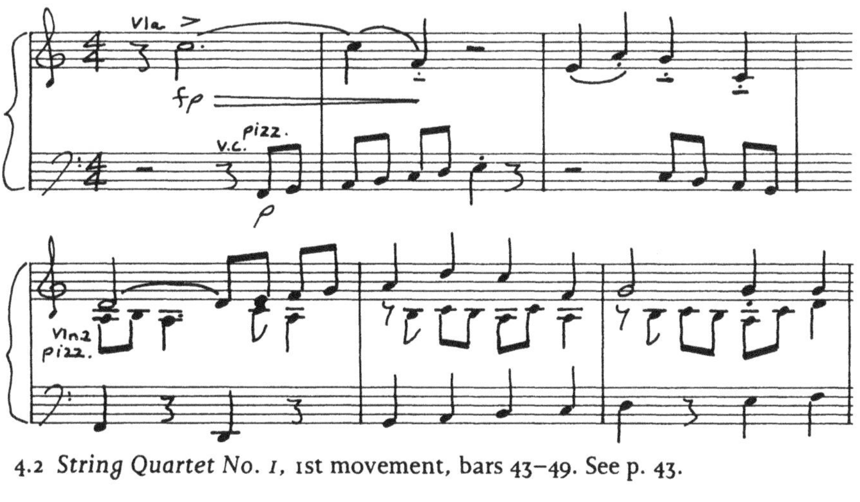

4.2 *String Quartet No. 1*, 1st movement, bars 43–49. See p. 43.

4.3 *String Quartet No. 1*, 1st movement, last 4 bars. See p. 44.

4.4 *String Quartet No. 1*, 1st movement, bars 32–35, 1st violin. See p. 44.

4.5 *String Quartet No. 1*, 2nd movement, bars 1–17. See p. 44.

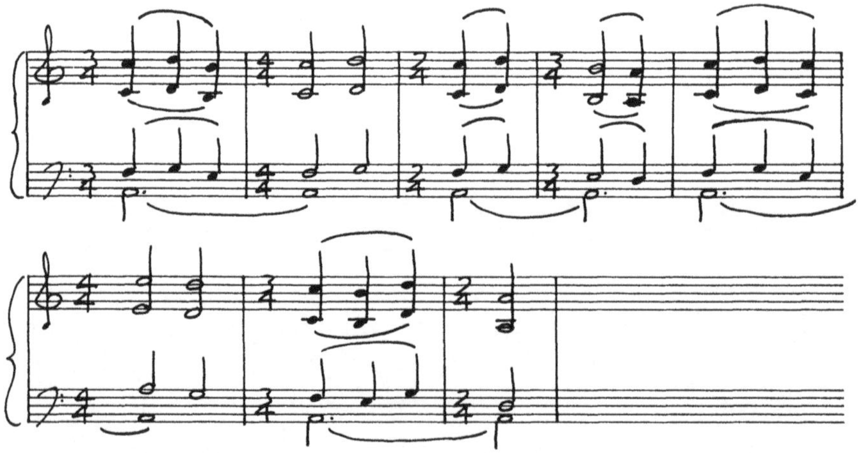

4.6 *String Quartet No. 1*, 2nd movement, bars 39–46. See p. 44.

4.7 *String Quartet No. 1*, 3rd movement, bars 1–12. See p. 44.

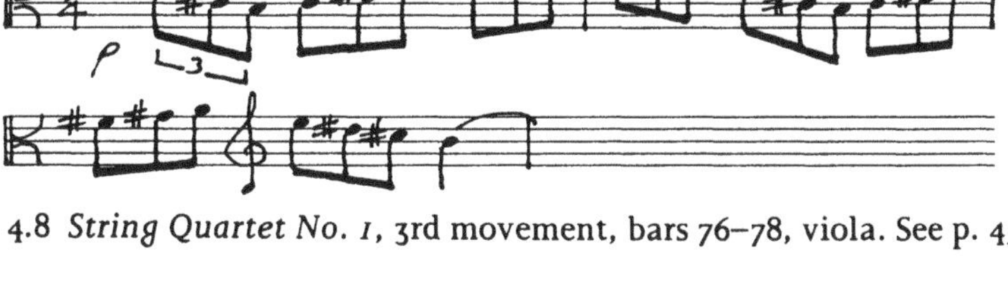

4.8 *String Quartet No. 1*, 3rd movement, bars 76–78, viola. See p. 45.

4.9 *Piano Sonata*, 1st movement, bars 1–19. See p. 46.

seen that the twelve-tone row could function divorced from the emotional expression used by Schoenberg.

String Quartet No. 1 (1944–5) is a good example of Pentland's style from that period, in which she combines traditional form with modern harmonic and melodic techniques. There are three movements, in the standard classical order of fast, slow, fast, that convey the standard attitudes of serious, lyrical, and light. The first movement follows the general outlines of classical first-movement form: it has two separate theme areas that complement one another in mood and shape, and the movement centres around their development and re-statement. The first theme (see Example 4.1) is introduced in unison and has three elements which become the basic motifs for development: a descending half-step followed by a step, used as the opening three notes of the composition; the skip of a sixth seen first in bar 2; and the rhythm presented as  in bar 1, and as  in bar 2. The characteristics of the second theme that are extracted for development are the initial, dramatic downward skip of a fifth, and the even motion of the quarter-note passages, both present in the viola part of Example 4.2.

Within this traditional format Pentland organizes the harmonic and melodic elements along more modern lines. The harmonic orientation of this quartet is one that she had been developing since her student days with Wagenaar – that of organization according to intervals rather than the traditional concept of tonality. At first the quartet would seem to relate to a traditional key. The opening bar singles out the notes E flat and C as important tones, and the movement ends on a clear C minor chord, which would suggest the tonality of C minor. But from the third bar forward the melodic and harmonic formations show that the composer is thinking in terms of intervals and not key or chord progressions; the first theme has G sharp and F sharp built in as essential notes, and any suggestion of traditional harmonic organization is completely erased when the second half of the first theme uses the same intervals as the first half, but a minor third higher (Example 4.1, end of bar 5). For the final full entry of the first theme the first violin plays an exact repeat of the opening ten bars as a method of melodic and 'tonal' unification, but here, as at all other structural points, there is no harmonic leading that would point towards a feeling of the tonality of C in the traditional sense. Instead, Pentland has used C as a basic note in a far more general sense. By its use at important structural points of the movement it takes on the function of 'tonic' in so far as it is the tonal focus. The note is singled out, however, not by a chordal sequence, as in traditional harmony, but by its melodic position which is supported by the intervals within the theme. At the end of the movement she uses the three motifs of the first theme to round off the form in the way it began (Example 4.3). The opening motif of descending half-step and step is presented in unison by the three lower instruments after first appearing ascending (E flat, F, G flat) in the first violin. The interval of a sixth is given in its original rhythmic formation, but a third higher (compare Example 4.2, bar 2) which leaves a sustained E flat over the closing C, G of the lower instruments, bringing back the C minor sound at the very end by means of intervallic relationships rather than chord leading.

In this movement Pentland has chosen a fairly lengthy first theme, but she has learned to drive her music forward by paring down the theme to a few essential motifs, and to spin out the line from these motifs. The most versatile motif in this movement is the rhythm ♩. ♪ ♩ and its variant noted above, which form a counter-melody that becomes a lyrical and more flexible line than either of the two principal themes (see Example 4.4).

In both the second and third movements Pentland further demonstrates her ability within the boundaries of the neo-classic. The neo-classicists of the early twentieth century, Hindemith among them, sought to rid themselves of nineteenth-century sounds by combining older forms, developmental techniques, and musical objectivity with a modern tonal freedom. The goal was to throw off the extreme emotionalism and pathos of the late Romantic movement in favour of the less emotional approach of the eighteenth century. Pentland's use of the neo-classic techniques and objectives in the second movement of the string quartet can be seen in the establishment of two distinct themes and their working out. The first theme is a wandering single line, treated in a contrapuntal fashion (see Example 4.5) and the second, which is skilfully derived from bar 3 of the first theme (see Example 4.6), is a more direct line with a narrow range and chordal treatment. Once the individual characters of the two themes are established the remainder of the movement is given to their combination and separation and an exchange of their characteristics to bring out their similarities and differences.

In the third movement a Bach-like driving theme is presented in the cello while the irregularity of the pizzicato accompaniment suggests the tongue-in-cheek treatment found occasionally in Prokofiev (see Example 4.7). The movement proceeds as a series of developments of various short motifs taken from the theme, with the entire theme returning in unison near the end. The most useful of the motifs, notes 5–8, resembles a cadence figure and is extremely flexible. Pentland employs a number of Bach techniques such as stretto and extension of a single rhythmic motif to build intensity, and conversion of the original duple theme to a triplet figure, as in Example 4.8, to lighten the spirit of the theme.

The overall achievement is true to the neo-classic ideal; all three movements have distinct and clearly heard traditional formal organizations that present classic, abstract characters: a serious sonata-form first movement, a lyrical song-like second movement, and a light, cheerful finale. The substitution of intervallic organization for traditional tonality, however, places the composition firmly in the twentieth century. But in addition to these general characteristics, Pentland includes stylistic ingredients distinctly her own. She has melded the intervallic ideas of Hindemith with her own version of textural and rhythmic lightness derived from Copland, and the resultant product is a unified style that is Pentland's.

It is also possible to see in this work two other characteristics of Pentland's early writing style that connect her with the neo-classic: the elements of pace and of texture. In imitation of the classical models, most of Pentland's works from this time proceed at a very regular pace. Beginning with the opening bars, each movement unfolds its material at a fairly steady rate, and from beginning to end the melodic and harmonic ideas are presented with regularity.

Pentland's idea of texture is also constant during this period and can be seen clearly in the quartet. Once the moving parts have all been introduced the number remains the same throughout the movement. In this case, all four instruments play most of the time, and the number of notes in the chords also remains fairly constant. The result of these two characteristics, the regularity both of pace and of texture, brings to Pentland's music a feeling of bulk and evenness, goals she had been taught at Juilliard. They would later be abandoned as she reoriented herself away from the neo-classic.

Throughout the early period Pentland's music is based on comparatively lengthy themes or, in some cases, full melodies. This can be seen even in those works based on a Baroque idea, such as in the third movement of the quartet (see Example 4.7). A part of the concept of thematic development, however, requires the breaking up of a theme into short motifs. This is one of the aspects of composition that Pentland continued to concentrate on throughout the period; more and more her themes were made up of short distinctive motifs. One advantage of the short motifs is that they are flexible and lend themselves to continual and imaginative working-out. Also, if the motifs are distinctive enough, the composer is able to make clear reference to the original theme without actually restating very much of it. With each succeeding work during the 1940s Pentland was changing in the direction of organizing her themes, and therefore her entire compositions, around motifs.

Piano Sonata (1945) exhibits this progressive move towards short motifs in a way that is almost prophetic of her later style. The theme of the first movement actually appears to grow as an extension of the short motifs found at the very beginning of the work. (See Example 4.9.) The movement begins by opposing two intervals in the first bar: a third and a second. As the bars proceed the two intervals are spun into longer and longer phrases until a theme results, beginning in bar 13. The interesting aspect of this movement is that it is made clear that the theme is a product of combining the two intervals, both melodically and, as initially stated, in harmonic opposition to one another. The other elements that Pentland chooses to develop in this movement are the short–long rhythm, found in its most elementary form in bar 1 and in a more developed way in bar 14, and the set of four evenly moving falling notes, bars 13 and 15.

A different aspect of Pentland's evolving interest in the smaller units of organization in her compositions can be seen in the second movement of the same sonata. The movement begins with a gentle, sad melody that fits easily into its 3/4 bars. The melody has a definite shape, but a closer look will reveal that the composer is very interested in the intervals of a second or ninth: B to C sharp in bars 1–2 and 4–5 (see Example 4.10). Development throughout the movement is built as much on this interval as it is on the thematic material, as in Examples 4.11 and 4.12 where the interval is developed melodically, or in 4.13 where it is used harmonically.

The sonata displays also another of Pentland's growing interests: unity between movements of the same work. In this case the reliance on very small motifs as the essence of each movement provides this unity. The three movements are related only on the level of the motifs: the intervals of a second and a third are present in all of them. In the second movement, in addition to the opposition of a second (ninth) at the beginning and end of the short phrases, the melody itself is made up of thirds. The third movement has also the basic opposition of a second, which is first presented as a seventh at the beginning and end of the first

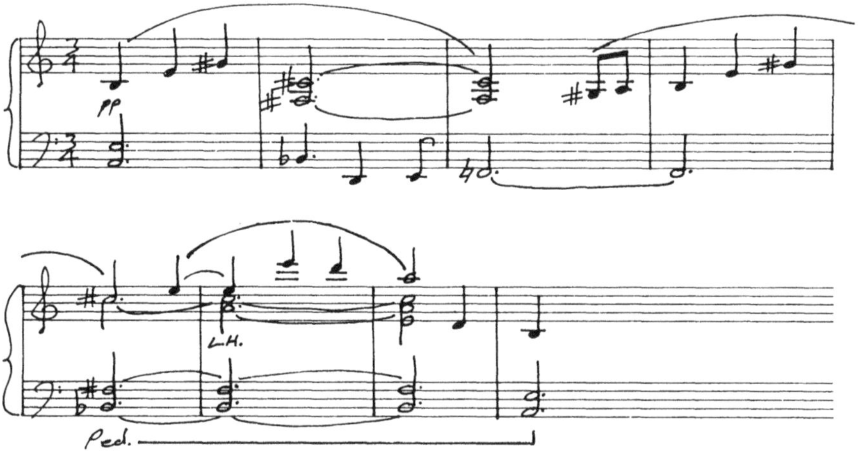

4.10 *Piano Sonata*, 2nd movement, bars 1–8. See p. 46.

4.11 *Piano Sonata*, 2nd movement, bars 46–47. See p. 46.

4.12 *Piano Sonata*, 2nd movement, bars 72–73. See p. 46.

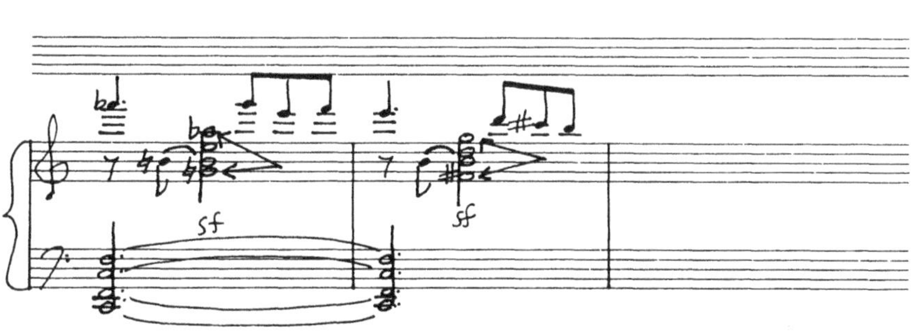

4.13 *Piano Sonata*, 2nd movement, bars 63–64. See p. 46.

4.14 *Piano Sonata*, 3rd movement, bars 1–8. See p. 47.

FOREST

4.15 *Song Cycle, Forest,* bars 1–14. See p. 47.

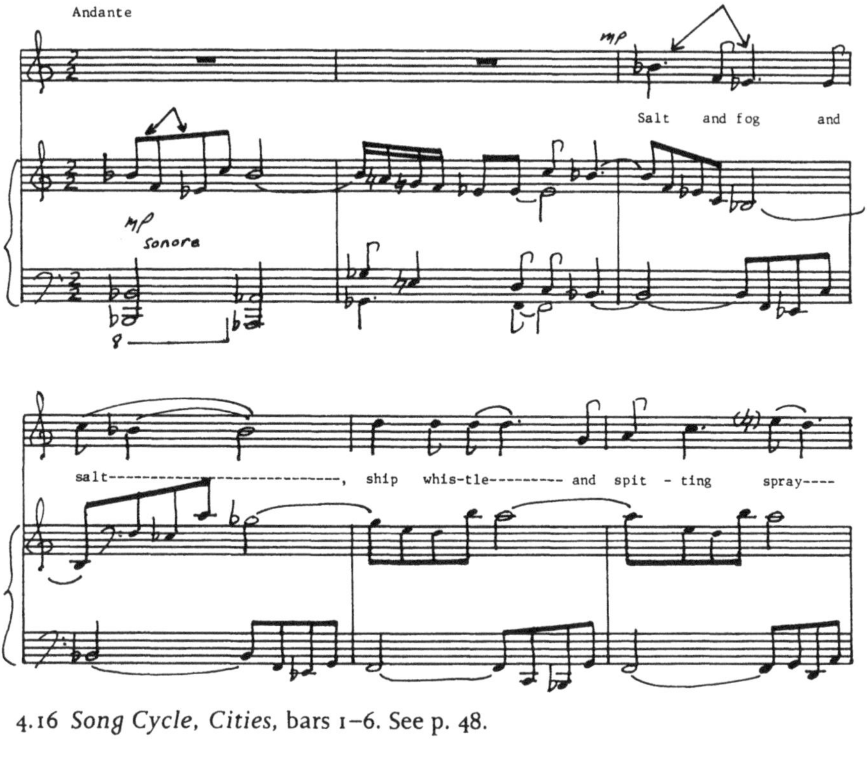

4.16 *Song Cycle, Cities,* bars 1–6. See p. 48.

4.17 *Song Cycle, Cities*, bars 17–24. See p. 48.

short phrase in bar 1. (See Example 4.14.) The interval of a third is used less obviously in this movement than in the other two, but it is found both harmonically and melodically throughout the movement.

As Pentland continued to work, her compositions give evidence of a constant search for ever tighter methods of organization. To her, the changes from one composition to the next made such an improvement that she was often embarrassed to hear one of her earlier works, thinking that the weaknesses were far too apparent to the listeners. Godfrey Ridout recalls presenting her *Piano Quartet* (1939) at an Art Gallery of Toronto concert in 1944. When he told Pentland it was to be played she became quite upset. She wanted to have her music performed, but at that time 'she always felt that every composition was weak except the one she just finished. We performed it and, of course, it was the best thing on the programme.'

One of the principal areas of her experimentation during the 1940s involved the shape and content of the thematic material. The change from lengthy melodies to short motifs can be seen on a large scale by comparing the thematic material in *String Quartet No. 1* with that in *Piano Sonata*. It is also present in miniature in the Marriott *Song Cycle*, which offers an opportunity to observe Pentland's gradual change of technique using the same format.

The cycle is a group of five poems by Anne Marriott set to music between December 1942 and July 1945. In the time between composing the first and last songs, Pentland made significant changes in her method of choosing and shaping themes. In the earliest-written song, *Forest*, the thematic material is comparatively lengthy and lacking in precise outline – characteristics that can be seen in all of her compositions up to this time. *Forest* has two basic themes: an angular and twisting line, seen in bars 1–6 of Example 4.15, that sets the mood of the text, with its gnarled shape and plodding manner portraying the imposing strength of the trees. The second theme, seen first in bars 6 and 7, is more a motif; it consists of the interval of a fifth used both harmonically in the piano accompaniment and melodically in the vocal part and suggests the majesty of the trees. Throughout the song these two elements, the wandering, shapeless melody and the fanfare-like fifth, are combined in a number of ways to unify the composition and to support the mood and sense of the text.

Forest exhibits all the aspects of Pentland's early style, including the economy of melodic material that always serves to produce a well-written composition; but she was not wholly content with the way in which she had chosen the melodic material. She had achieved what she intended to do aesthetically with *Forest*: to portray the text with combinations of two opposing thematic ideas, and yet she felt a need for more unity. Perhaps it was at this point that she reflected on Copland's practice of deriving an entire composition from a small motif stated at the beginning of a work. She had imitated that technique successfully in her *Variations for Piano* (January 1942; discussed in chapter 3), and a year later we can see her experimenting with that very technique as a means of more tightly unifying the remaining four songs in *Cycle*. By the time she completed the last song, *Cities*, she had advanced a noticeable distance in that regard.

Cities has two motifs: the first is the five-note pattern  seen in the first bar of Example 4.16, and the other is a descending scale, seen in bar 23 of Example 4.17. The most obvious change from the motifs in the first song of the cycle is that here both motifs are short and have a distinctive shape that makes them easily identifiable – a Copland trait. Pentland has also taken another hint from her teacher in that both motifs have an essential element in common – the structural interval of a fifth. The relationship of the two motifs is strengthened by the appearance of the second motif in bar 2 (see Example 4.16), where it initially appears to be no more than the filling-in of the first motif. The motifs themselves, their rhythmic working out, and their harmonies all support the mood and images of the text, just as the two longer and unrelated themes had done in *Forest*. In the two and a half years that had elapsed between the two songs Pentland had refined a technique of unification through the use of a single basic interval that is given different motivic shapes. The short melodic-rhythmic motifs are then expanded and varied to give the music an underlying unity that is not apparent on first hearing. This technique brings a new depth to the composition and attests to Pentland's growing control of her craft.

During the early 1940s Canada attempted to encourage good relations with the Soviet Union through the National Council for Canadian-Soviet Friendship. A part of the program involved an exchange of music from the two countries and Pentland became involved as composer, performer, and arranger. Her *Arioso and Rondo*, *Rhapsody 1939*, and *Studies in Line* were performed in Russia along with compositions by other Canadians, and on the other half of the exchange several Canadian-Soviet concerts took place in Toronto, also featuring works by composers from both countries. *Studies in Line* was performed again on the July 1944 program and Harry Adaskin played the violin concerto on the series in March 1945, shortly after he played its première; and in February a small ensemble from the Toronto Symphony performed Yuri Shaporin's *The Birth of Russia*, orchestrated by Pentland.

After one of the performances in the Soviet-Canadian series Pentland was asked by a member of the Soviet Communist party why she did not write music that was more accessible to the 'people.' Her reply was that she felt it was more important to write music to please herself. She was attracted to Soviet music, but her conception of politics and of her role in society was another thing entirely. She could in no way consider writing to please the 'masses'; to do that would be to follow, not to lead.

She was not indifferent to having an audience for her works – far from it. In an essay she wrote in 1947 for a program by the Jewish Folk Choir in Toronto she pleads directly for an audience, but on her own terms. She suggests that concert programming was controlled by consideration of those compositions that have already proven to draw a large audience. 'The Box Office has a dictator's grip on the public mind, which it lulls into a semi-quiescent state so that it may be set in the one listening groove which pays.' She argues that the modern composer should not compromise by way of writing in the styles of the past. 'Much as we admire and learn from the old masters, we cannot afford to live mentally in the past, if only for the sake of our obligations to the future.' Her point is that an effort must be made to expose the listening public to the music of its era: 'We [contemporary composers] have something to say. [But] most of that remains in cold storage.'

She wanted Canadian performers and producers to present a variety of modern music as well as older music in concert. In her opinion, the modern composers were not given a chance to attract the interest of the audience, and unless something were done to change this, Canadian composers would not continue to develop and Canadian music would soon loose contact with the rest of the modern world. Her position was the antithesis of that of her Soviet questioner: she felt it was her duty to stay current in terms of her compositional approach. To give in to the 'masses' by producing what they were used to hearing would be to abdicate her role and to become artistically dishonest.

In 1945 Pentland finally tried her hand at a symphony. Up to this point she had written only programmatic orchestral music for radio and extended works for chamber ensembles. The large symphonic form and the large orchestra for which it is written traditionally have different requirements from the short songs and intimate chamber works we have already looked at. Instead of the fine and subtle detail, the symphonic form calls for clearly stated thematic material and broad gestures that take advantage of the many colours and contrasts available from the ensemble.

Symphony No. 1 was written over a relatively long period, 1945–8, and is dedicated to the memory of Cécile Gauthiez, who died in 1944, although there is no trace of Gauthiez's influence in it. *Symphony No. 1* is another of Pentland's neo-classic compositions that uses the traditional form with modern sounds. All four movements use traditional forms and motifs rather than full melodies: the first, *Largo tranquillo*, has two contrasting themes shaped into a sonata form; the second and third are both related to Baroque dance ideas – the second, *Allegro giocoso*, has a drone-like accompaniment figure similar to a *musette*, and the third, *Adagio sostenuto*, has the melodic phrases and rhythmic patterns of a *saraband*; and the fourth, *Allegro animato*, is a series of short motifs in rondo form based on a single rhythmic idea. It is interesting to see the way in which Pentland adapts her new motivic ideas to the demands of the larger form.

The symphony begins with an introduction section in which the basic thematic material of the entire work is stated. Within the first three bars the essential intervals, rhythms, and melodic shapes are presented (Example 4.18). A different set of elements is emphasized in each of the themes throughout the symphony, but all of them are elaborations of the material presented in the first three bars. This is not a new technique; a similar idea can be found in the late symphonies of Haydn, but there are problems in adjusting the idea to the modern style.

Theme 1 of the first movement (Example 4.19) is quite close to the introductory material. The note sequence is almost identical for two bars, and the remainder of the theme is an elaboration of a number of the intervals and rhythms of the introduction. The dramatic, jolting rhythm of the introductory bars is transformed into a sweeping, long-lined theme, driven forward by the rhythmic figure ♫♪♩. Throughout the movement the reshaping and development of the first theme always include the ♫♪♩ rhythm and the interval of an octave; the octave is found as an important interval in each of the themes.

Theme 2 (Example 4.20) is also rather lengthy, and, in contrast to the bright and active first theme, it is slower-moving and tranquil. The intervals and rhythms are taken from the introductory material, but the only obvious element it shares with theme 1 is the prominent use of the octave. The entire working out of the first movement is based on the general outlines of sonata form, with the two contrasting themes

4.18 *Symphony No. 1*, 1st movement, bars 1–3, bass. See p. 50.

4.19 *Symphony No. 1*, 1st movement, bars 34–44, strings. See p. 50.

4.20 *Symphony No. 1*, 1st movement, bars 55–64, flute. See p. 50.

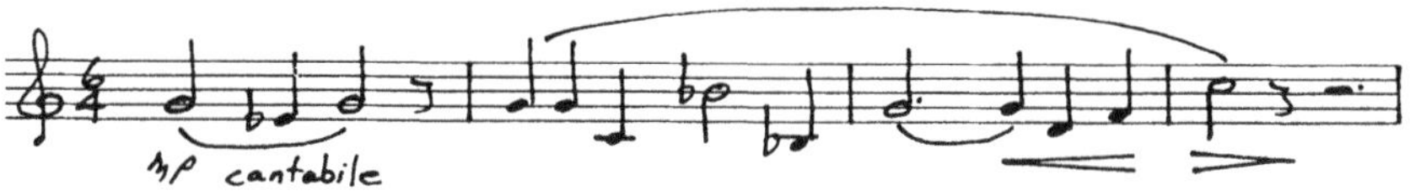

4.21 *Symphony No. 1*, 3rd movement, bars 1–4, trumpet. See p. 51.

4.22 *Symphony No. 1*, 3rd movement, bars 8–12, first violin; bars 59–64, flute; bars 71–73, cello. See p. 51.

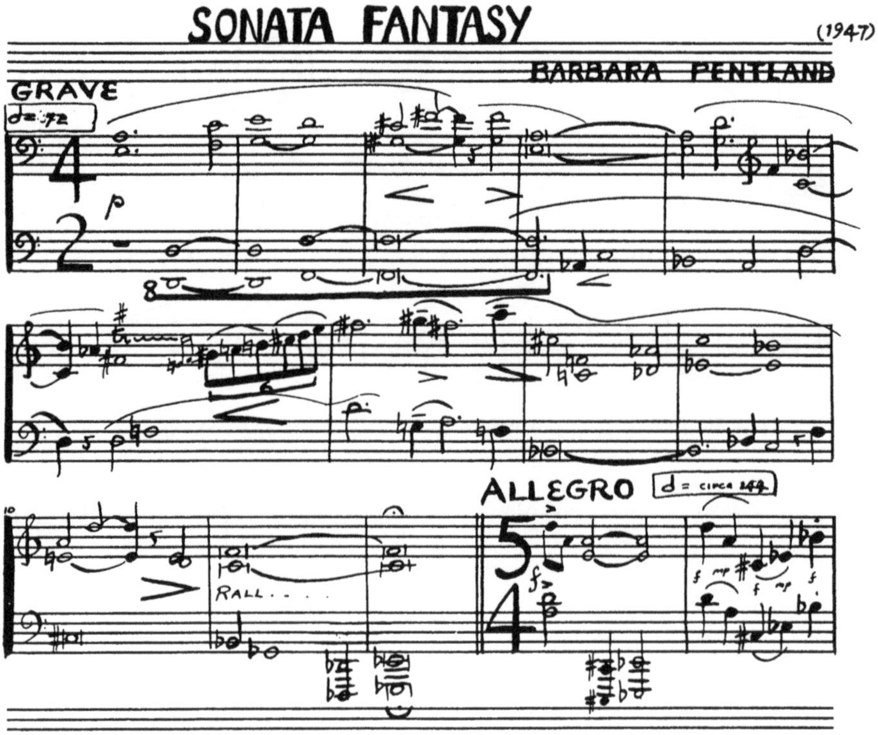

4.23 *Sonata Fantasy*, bars 1–14. See p. 52.

4.24 *Sonata Fantasy*, bars 244–255. See p. 52.

demonstrating both the energetic and the relaxed potential of the basic intervallic source material.

The third movement demonstrates a different approach to melody and form. It too draws on the introductory material for its basic elements, but instead of contrasting two themes as in the first movement, the entire third movement is a series of constantly changing phrases, all based on the rhythms and general melodic curve of the opening four bars (seen in Example 4.21). The initial phrase is rarely repeated exactly but there is no doubt that all the phrases are derived from it. Example 4.22 shows a few of the variations found throughout the movement. If the movement were to be given a formal name, therefore, it would be 'quasi-theme and variations' or, more correctly, 'motif and variations,' a technique related to that found in many of the instrumental works of Bach, for example, his unaccompanied violin works.

Each movement of the symphony maintains an evenness of pace that gives the work a directness and sense of relentless motion that is typical of all Pentland's work from this period. She has adjusted her technique to take advantage of the various sound potentials of the orchestra, however, including the extremes of volume and the many instrument colours. Her orchestration shows an awareness of the variety of sound colours available in the full orchestra, and she combines the instruments with skill. Her desire for even motion causes her to maintain an instrument combination for sixteen bars or longer, but she varies the texture frequently from many instruments to a combination of soloists, introducing a new sense of texture variation not seen in earlier works.

Little by little in the works of this period Pentland was headed in the direction of thematic economy. She was unifying her compositions by reducing the quantity of essential ingredients and retaining variety by creatively rearranging these few basic ingredients. With the third movement of the symphony she had even gone to the point of using not a theme but a motif that remains in a constant state of development.

The differences between this composition and the chamber works we have examined have to do with the quantity of material and the way in which it is presented. In *String Quartet No. 1* and *Song Cycle* for example, a relatively large number of variations of the basic motifs are used. The motivic elements are constantly recombined and given rather subtle variation. Pentland's chamber music technique from this period deals with attention to detail on a small plane, requiring the close attention of the listener. In the symphony the elements are used on a larger scale. The themes are longer, their characteristic elements are more distinctive, and they are presented in a less complex manner – generally brought out one at a time and clearly audible. As we follow the development of Pentland's style we will see that one of the changes involves the use of the more detailed treatment in the larger compositions.

Pentland's early mature compositional style is best summed up in her *Sonata Fantasy* (1947). In it she calls upon all the technical approaches she had synthesized from both Hindemith and Copland. It is the summation of her early style yet points the way to the next major change. It is a model of the combination of two classical forms set in a twentieth-century idiom – a gem of neo-classic writing. It deserves the same degree of popularity given to *Studies in Line*. Although in many respects the two compositions are quite different, they both exhibit a vitality and conciseness of statement that is Pentland at her best.

Sonata Fantasy cleverly combines both sonata form and fugue in a single, continuous movement. The first theme (Example 4.23) begins with an ascending melodic motion of thirds in slow motion with the harmonic opposition of a ninth (sixteenth) always prominent. The second theme is a contrast in tempo and melodic direction (bar 13), and it is the expansion of this theme that eventually becomes a full fugue at bar 244. (See Example 4.24.) The overall form is that of the classical statement, development, and recapitulation, with the fugue serving as the development of the second theme. By means of the development the listener is slowly made aware of the actual economy of material. Although the two themes have contrasting melodic shapes, their initial melodic and harmonic intervals are very much the same; both themes begin with the interval of a fourth and a ninth. The composition is more tightly controlled than previous works because, although the two themes are fairly long in their full forms, the initial intervals that they have in common are the portions the composer uses most of the time for the purpose of development and transition.

The harmonic scheme shows Hindemith's principle of overall intervallic concept. The tonal reference is founded on the same principle of organization as described earlier in the discussion of *String Quartet No. 1*. Throughout *Sonata Fantasy* there is constant reference back to the opening tones on E, A, and D, at such important structural places as the middle of the work just prior to the fugue, the recapitulation section (bar 488), and the final bars. Between these points of solid tonal reference the actual notes on which the thematic material appears are dictated only by intervallic principles rather than by any harmonic scheme. The work is driven forward by a spinning-out of the various intervals found in the two themes, a fully Baroque technique. The eighteenth-century master carefully accompanied spinning-out by a series of temporary modulations from key to key in order to accommodate his tonal motifs; Pentland's work has a similar organization. The line is moved forward by progression from one statement of the motifs to another, while the harmonic accompaniment continues to use the intervals introduced at the beginning of the work. The intervals of the motifs determine the pitch at which the next motif will begin, and the harmonies remain in the same relationship to them. The harmonic and melodic motifs spring from a common well, and therefore, regardless of the beginning pitch of the new motivic statement, the other voices retain the harmonic intervals found in the original statement of the composition. The parallel with Baroque music does not end here; Pentland shows also her own mastery of the twentieth-century harmonic idiom by taking the fugue subject through a systematic tour of the chromatic scale. From the time the fugue treatment begins until it ends at the recapitulation, each entry begins on a successively higher step of the chromatic scale until all twelve steps have been used as entry points.

Sonata Fantasy is a tour de force for Pentland in that it shows facility and complete mastery of the technique she had been developing through the decade. More than any other work of this period it has a tightness and economy of technique, and it transmits to the listener the same degree of drama and strength as the classical forms she has so ably imitated.

While *Sonata Fantasy* is a model of twentieth-century neo-classicism, several of its elements point the way to Pentland's future style. Her future compositions can be seen in the vigorous and angular thematic lines; the short, easily recognized intervallic motifs; and the serial nature of the fugue theme. Until this work, Pentland's melodic lines had been somewhat smoother and more step-wise. Although the smooth melodic lines were easy to work with because the smoothness gave them plasticity, to imbue them with energy required relatively lengthy rhythmic development, as seen in *String Quartet No. 1* and *Symphony No. 1*. The angular nature of the theme in *Sonata Fantasy*, however, contained this energy in a much shorter space. In the fugue subject Pentland for the first time approached the serial technique that had attracted her since her student days; the subject of the fugue has a ten-note row. (See Example 4.24.) Her use of row was not strict in this work, and has never been so, but she could see the advantage; it offered an economy that suited her evolving style. The row allowed a more rational control of the melodic and harmonic elements in the style she wanted to continue to develop.

Her style from the 1940s can be classified generally as neo-classic: having traditional forms with modern melodic and harmonic sounds, and without the nineteenth-century extremes of emotionalism. But this is a very loose description of her work. The compositions include a great deal of variety – works for voice, orchestra, chamber ensemble, and soloists – and no two are alike. In all her work she aimed for linear clarity, and as the decade progressed she moved more and more in the direction of short motifs spun out in a Baroque fashion to achieve this. A 1948 article in the *International Musician* more colourfully described her music by noting that she is from the prairies and that her music 'reflects long line and lean texture, presenting an uncluttered landscape' (13).

In the seven years following her first summer in Tanglewood, Pentland had made her mark and established herself as one of the leading composers in Canada. Her compositions were played with increasing frequency in Canada and elsewhere, and she was building an international reputation. Her move to Toronto was certainly a big help in presenting the right opportunities, but the groundwork had been firmly laid before she moved. Her Toronto success was the result of a long and arduous preparation. She had spent years of persistent effort learning the techniques of her craft, so that when the opportunities presented themselves in Toronto she was able to take advantage of them. By 1941 she had established a style of writing, seen in *Studies in Line*, that is clearly her own, but even earlier she had produced music of obvious quality such as *Five Preludes* in 1938 and *Piano Quartet* and *Lament* in 1939. What she needed was an opportunity to receive a fair hearing for her compositions, and Toronto in the 1940s was the right place for that. When she first arrived in Toronto the scene was set for the awakening of interest in modern music, and she was prepared and willing to help it develop. In turn, the performances, criticism, and the opportunity to associate with other modern artists helped her continue to grow.

5

Transition 1948–1955

Pentland's continued search for tighter control over her compositions finally led her to investigate the potential of serial technique. In her 1943 article she had mentioned the technique in passing, but rejected it because of the emotionalism she found in the music of the most famous serial composer, Arnold Schoenberg. Her Toronto colleague, Weinzweig, used the technique, however, and she could see that emotionalism was not a necessary part. By the late 1940s her own technique was obviously gravitating in that direction in the same way and for the same reasons Schoenberg's had in the early years of the century. Both of them consciously rejected the harmonic system of the nineteenth century and wanted to establish a system in which all notes of the scale had more equality and independence. For Pentland there had been a gradual but direct line away from the traditional harmonic orientation of her very early works, towards one of dependence on the interval only, with an equality among the notes that was not available in the traditional system. The first big step along the path was the adoption of Hindemith's idea of interval independence which had its basis in the overtone system. Thinking of her compositions along the lines of intervals alone worked very well for Pentland, and she refined that technique throughout the 1940s. But we can see in the ten-note row of the fugue subject of *Sonata Fantasy* that the independence of the intervals, together with her ideas of motivic generation of theme, was leading her directly towards many of the basic tenets of serial technique.

Pentland is very methodical, and she did not embrace the system of serial composition all at once. She had known a bit about it since her student days at Juilliard, and her association with Weinzweig gave her additional insights, but the actual change of orientation took place after a rather lengthy transition period during which she carefully integrated some of the basic ideas of serialism with the technique she had been using. The change was actually quite a natural one, since by 1947 she was already well along in that direction. On reflection now she can see how Schoenberg came upon his method, and she suggests that, had there not already been a method of twelve-tone composition by 1950, she probably would have developed a comparable one as the result of her own search; and on the basis of what was happening in her compositions of the late 1940s the statement seems accurate.

If there was a formal start to the change of techniques it was the two summers Pentland spent in New Hampshire at the MacDowell Colony. The colony is an isolated retreat for artists and writers, founded by the widow of composer Edward MacDowell, and Pentland went there in the summer of 1947 for a change of scene and a break from the active life in Toronto. Dika Newlin, once a student of Arnold Schoenberg, was there, working on her translation of René Leibowitz's *Schoenberg et son école*, and through conversation with Newlin, Pentland learned more about Schoenberg's theories.

The two summers in New Hampshire were very pleasant for Pentland. She had a studio deep in the woods complete with a grand piano, fireplace, and veranda. Lunch was brought out to the studios by car, which enabled her to work uninterrupted all day. Besides the rustic beauty of the New England countryside, there were relaxing hours playing four-hand piano with Newlin and the excitement of learning the details of serial technique. The musicians at the colony were unevenly divided in their allegiance: everyone else was studying and imitating Stravinsky's style, which defined the position of Newlin and Pentland all the more clearly as that of the 'opposing' Schoenbergian camp, a rather curious position for Pentland, given her earlier rejection of the system. But by then she had moved some distance from her 1943 opinion, and the details of the system as elucidated by Newlin were becoming more attractive.

Colony Music: Overture, Chorale, Burlesque was begun and completed in 1947, but although it was written during the time she was becoming acquainted with the serial technique, there is no sign of that technique in the composition. It is a very happy work, reflecting her pleasant experience at the colony; a three-movement divertimento that does contain the new trend towards shorter and more angular motifs seen in her compositions of the mid-1940s, but the harmonic plan is the one derived from Hindemith, i.e. overall tonal shape with the intervals of the motifs determining the pitches used.

The first work in which Pentland seriously adopted the serial technique for an entire composition is *Octet for Winds* (1948). This perhaps should mark the beginning of Pentland's second period, but in fact it does not; her change to a new style was more gradual than that and occurred in 1955 after an additional influence. Instead, *Octet* marks the beginning of a transition; a setting of the stage for the second style. The composition was begun during the second summer at the MacDowell Colony, after Pentland had spent a year thinking through the technique of serial composition and was able to consult Newlin on the finer points. But *Octet* really does not act like a serial composition in terms of either Schoenberg's works or those of Pentland's second style. As a matter of fact, it is difficult to find in it a clear and direct statement of a row without a number of tone repetitions. The melodic segments appear to be based on perhaps a ten-note series (as can be seen in the trombone part, Example 5.1). The overall effect, though, is not the Schoenbergian control of note sequence, but Hindemith's ideal of important structural tonal centres, with the notes E flat and B flat appearing in most of the important structural locations, such as the beginning of the work, the end, the first and second phrase cadences, and all of the sectional beginnings. (See Example 5.2.) Pentland's original intention may have been to allow the serial technique to play an important part in the formation of the work, but it is so heavily dependent on the principle of intervallic outline and structural tones that, although Pentland considers it her first serial composition, it is really one of the works most closely related to the Hindemith approach.

These were important years of development and change for music and musicians in Canada. The efforts of the young composers were having a strong effect on Canadian music. Pentland, Weinzweig, and others were disturbing the complacent musical public, not only with their music, but also in radio interviews, the daily press, and journal articles, where they spoke out, challenging the audience to give modern music a fair hearing. A series of events beginning in the late 1940s brought the young composers and their music to prominence. First, several of them were given university positions: Barbara Pentland at the University of British Columbia and István Anhalt at McGill in 1949, John Weinzweig at the University of Toronto (to replace Healey Willan and Leo Smith, who retired in 1950), Jean Papineau-Couture at the Université de Montréal in 1951, and Murray Adaskin at the University of Saskatchewan in 1952.

The Canadian League of Composers was established in 1951, and the Canada Council in 1957, a source of financial aid to creative artists (*CM* 34).

Harry Adaskin had been appointed head of the department of music at the University of British Columbia in 1946, and in the summer of 1949 he invited Pentland to join the faculty to teach twentieth-century composition techniques. This, of course, would mean leaving the city of so many musical successes for Pentland, but for all of its artistic advantages, Toronto did not offer her a steady income. The conservatory position was on a commission basis,which was fairly hazardous, and although the influx of veterans after the war had provided her with a number of pupils, the government rehabilitation program was coming to an end. She had been offered positions at other universities in the past: Queen's in 1945, Mount Holyoke College in Massachusetts in 1946, and (as a temporary replacement for Newlin) Western Maryland College in 1949; but she turned them down for various reasons. This offer was different; the appointment was a permanent one and she was to be given a free hand in designing the theory courses. The decision was made quickly, and by August 1949 Pentland had moved to Vancouver and settled into a left-over wartime hut on the campus grounds.

She quickly earned a reputation as a good but demanding teacher. She had definite views about standards and would not tolerate sloppy work from her students. She insisted that the composing students acquire a firm background in traditional techniques and keep an open mind to new ideas. When they made the usual error of hiding behind complex chromatic chords and excessive melodies she would send them home with five notes with which to write their next assignment; once they had learned discipline and economy they would be permitted more notes. Her students remember her as a very positive influence. H. Colin Slim, now professor of music at the University of California at Irvine, credits Pentland with giving him a thorough background in theory, and Robert Rogers, an active performer and teacher in Vancouver who has performed much of Pentland's music over the last decades, speaks highly of her classes in traditional harmony and analysis.

Even to the UBC students not in her class she was known as one of the most dynamic professors on the campus. They would watch her in awe as she walked across the campus, always with long, hurried strides, head down, her mind obviously on some serious problem. Her sense of purpose was communicated to everyone, and some attended her recitals just to be in the presence of so powerful a personality.

Life in Vancouver was much quieter. There was little that compared to the avant-garde circle she had enjoyed in Toronto. The Adaskins continued to offer her friendship just as they had in Toronto, however, and with their help she settled into her new position. As a result of their efforts and enthusiasm for her music, her compositions were soon heard on a number of concert programs in and around Vancouver, and she continued to be a popular guest at conferences and symposia, in British Columbia and elsewhere. She appeared on the CBC broadcast from Toronto in 1950 'An Investigation of Modernism in the Arts' along with Robertson Davies, Abraham Klein, and Jacques de Tonnancour.

As we look back now, we can see that during this period Pentland was undertaking an intensive search to reconcile the techniques of her early mature period with the new technique she had decided to adopt. By this time she had already established the fundamentals of her own style; she had worked out her own approach to form and her concept of melodic and rhythmic development. Perhaps the real problem was that she had established a fairly clear personal concept of melody and harmony, and the struggle was to incorporate the elements of the new technique into an already well-developed style. Throughout the 1940s the intervallic technique had worked quite well for her, as evidenced by a number of her finest compositions. And yet she felt something lacking – an element of harmonic control and formal integration that she needed. The Schoenberg idea of composition from the twelve-tone row appealed to her; it provided exactly that control she had wanted. But in spite of her strong attraction to the technique, she hesitated to embrace the entire theory; she was more of a lyricist than the strict observation of serial technique would allow when combined with the other elements of her technique. By examining some of the works written during the period 1948–54, we can trace her efforts to find just those elements of the serial technique that would give her the tonal control she needed, while at the same time allowing her the freedom to be spontaneous.

Symphony No. 2 (1950) can be described in much the same way as *Octet*; it possesses both an overall tonal plot and a tone series – a clear mixture of the old and the new techniques. The first movement is full of energy generated from short motifs that are found in the very first bar (see Example 5.3). The two important motifs are the four-note fanfare-like group on beats 1 and 2, containing a skip of a fourth, and a two-note motif in the bass on beat 4, made up of a short–long rhythm and the interval of a step. From these two contrasting rhythms and intervals and the interval of a sixth (seen in only its harmonic form in bar 1, B flat–G), Pentland assembles the entire movement. There is no clear theme in this work in the sense of a fully shaped melodic phrase. The lyrical passages are formed by linking the motifs into longer phrases, as in bars 14 and 15 of Example 5.3, or by using the basic intervals of the three motifs, a fourth, sixth, and second, to construct a contrasting phrase, as in Example 5.4.

The use of serial technique in this movement is fairly loose. By the end of the opening phrase in bar 12, all twelve notes of the series have been used (compare Example 5.3 with Example 5.5), but the tones are added gradually, with a large amount of repetition. Especially clear is the note G which opens and closes the phrase and appears at a number of important structural points throughout the movement, including the last note (see Example 5.6).

In these last bars of the movement she returns to her source motifs and sums up the work by sounding all the essential ingredients: the fanfare motif melodically against the harmonic background of the second, with the interval of a sixth (here inverted to a third) in the outside voices.

The other three movements of *Symphony No. 2* are related to the first through a clever realignment of the essential motivic material. The second movement emphasizes the inversion of the intervals found in the first movement; the fourth becomes a fifth, and the sixth is inverted to a third (see Example 5.7), and in place of the major second, in this movement there is the minor second (C sharp–D in bars 4–5). In the third movement the intervals are a fourth, a third, and a seventh (see Example 5.8), and in the fourth movement, a third, a minor second (see Example 5.9), and eventually the fourth. In all the movements a common tone series can be found, but it is never any more directly stated than in the first movement. At this point in her development the series was an aid in controlling the harmonic and melodic flow within the individual phrases, but it was not used to form the overall plan of a complete movement.

In looking at *Symphony No. 2* from the point of view of musical expression, we can see that Pentland has used the broad gestures seen in *Symphony No. 1*. Each movement presents a single and separate mood; the dramatic fanfare motif and the more lyrical phrases in the first movement all have the singular spirit of a direct and vigorous mood. (See Example 5.3.) The general attitude of this movement is one of bright energy, which is caused by the kinds of motifs chosen, the orchestration, which is bright, and the constant regular rhythms which suggest a dance in the order of a tarantella.

5.1 *Octet for Winds*. See p. 57.

5.2 *Octet for Winds*, bars 1–9. See p. 57.

Allegro ♩. = 120-144

5.3 *Symphony No. 2*, 1st movement, bars 1–15. See p. 59.

5.4 *Symphony No. 2*, 1st movement, bars 24–31. See p. 60.

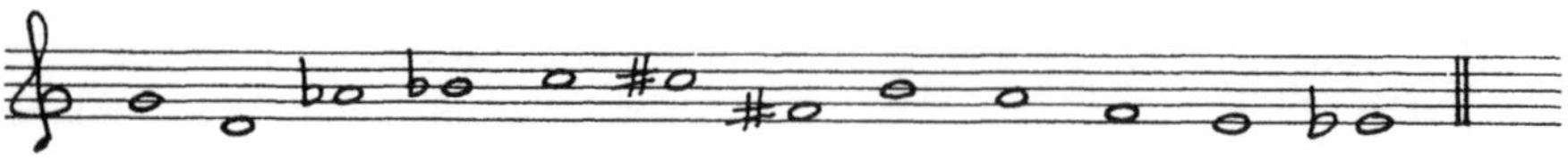

5.5 *Symphony No. 2*, 1st movement, tone row. See p. 60.

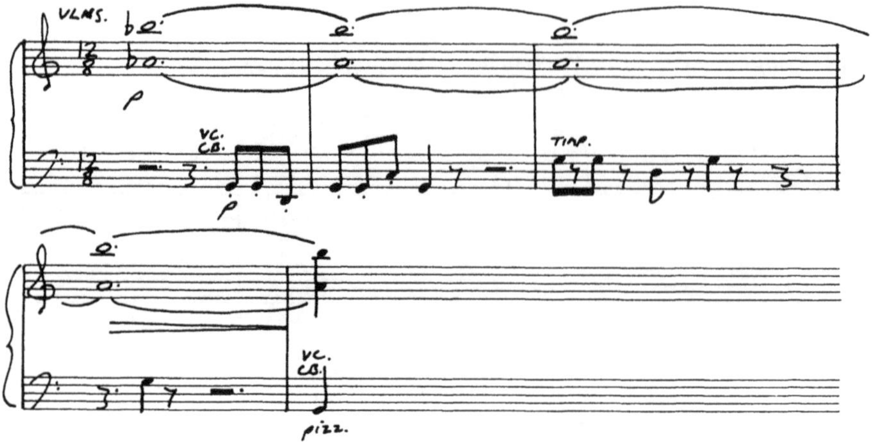

5.6 *Symphony No. 2*, 1st movement, bars 160–164. See p. 60.

5.7 *Symphony No. 2*, 2nd movement, bars 1–7. See p. 60.

5.8 *Symphony No. 2*, 3rd movement, bars 2–4. See p. 60.

5.9 *Symphony No. 2*, 4th movement, bars 1–11. See p. 60.

5.10 *The Lake*, bars 141–144. See p. 62.

In the second movement, the expression is completely different, although the intervals are closely related to those of the first. In place of the firm and direct statements of the first movement, here there is a definite effort to be indirect and unforceful. The constant occurrence of half-steps in the melodic flow brings out an attitude of indecisiveness which is reinforced by phrases that wander off rather than conclude, or just stop and start without definition.

The third movement is as close to a dance as anything Pentland has written. This is by intention – the marking is 'Tempo da samba' – and there is a suggestion of Copland in the rhythms and the lightness of the orchestration. And for the fourth movement there is a rousing, forceful, and brilliantly scored presto based on the driving force of the rhythm ♪ ♩, reminiscent of a motif in the first movement, that is preceded by a Beethoven-like dramatic introduction.

As a whole, *Symphony No. 2* presents four completely different musical moods. The angular and indecisive second movement is an effective contrast to the other three movements, all of which are direct and rhythmically active. The only material relationship between the movements is through the intervals chosen as the basic source of the melodies and harmonies. The twelve-tone series is used in the work, and its presence insures at least the use of all twelve tones before the end of the opening section of each movement, but this is a very loose application of the serial technique. The essential generative source of the music and its point of unity is a set of intervals that are taken from the row and given melodic and rhythmic elaboration.

Pentland's only opera, *The Lake* (1952), also was finished during this period. The work was originally to be a commission by a London, Ontario, lawyer and amateur organist, Gordon Jeffery. Jeffery, with Ernest White, had earlier commissioned *Concerto for Organ and Strings* (1949), which they premièred in April 1951 with success. Shortly afterwards Jeffery again wrote to Pentland and requested a 'Canadian Chamber Opera, if possible to a Canadian libretto, and for a modest group of singers and players.' He further stated that the performers he had in mind were a highly trained bass and soprano with dramatic experience; a fair tenor with no dramatic ability; and a contralto with a fine voice. The opera was to have only a single scene, allowing a concert performance, approximately twenty-four minutes in duration.

Pentland accepted the commission and the limitations and approached Dorothy Livesay for a libretto. Livesay suggested the Indian legend of Ogopogo, the monster of Lake Okanagan, because she was in possession of some original material on the subject. The plot contrasts the world of the white settlers with that of the Okanagan Indians. It deals with the incidents surrounding the first sighting in 1874 by a white person of the mythical lake monster. To heighten their sense of the story Pentland and Livesay spent several weeks in the area visiting the cabin where the incident took place and talking with people who had known the family.

In keeping with the guidelines of the commission, the opera has four characters: Susan Allison (soprano), pioneer housewife; her husband John Allison (bass), pioneer English cattleman; Marie (contralto), an elderly Indian woman, child-nurse and domestic to Mrs Allison; and Johnny MacDougall (tenor), Scottish-Indian half-breed, guide and handyman. The single scene takes place in front of the Allisons' log cabin. Susan implores her husband not to take a trip across the lake because there is a storm and she has a premonition of danger. He chides her for being influenced by the old Indian tales and departs, but the storm forces his boat to shore. Marie and Johnny believe it was the lake monster, not the wind, that pushed the boat, and they convince Susan. John is not persuaded to believe in the existence of the monster, and the opera ends with all four principals singing of their hope for the new land.

To set the text, Pentland wrote for an orchestra as specified in the commission, of flute, oboe, trumpet, piano, and eleven strings (string quartet in the revised version of 1977). She handles this comparatively small orchestra and vocal quartet in a style half-way between her broad style as seen in *Symphony No. 2* and the more detailed style she uses in her chamber and solo works. One of the major motifs in the opera is a rhythm derived from the speech rhythm of the name of the lake monster, Na-aitka, which is set to the rhythm ♪ ♩. ♪ ♪, usually with a half-step on the first two syllables and the same pitch for the last two, as in Example 5.10. The accompaniment, as seen in the same example in its simplest form, is a static rhythm derived from the vocal motif for Na-aitka. This rhythm from the vocal part is used each time the name of the monster is mentioned, and the accompaniment rhythm is used as a broad leitmotif whenever the monster is spoken of directly, and even, as in Example 5.11, when it is suggested or implied in the dialogue. In this case the text refers to the monster, and the rhythmic motif reinforces the reference. The only variation to this use of leitmotif takes place in the episode where Susan and Marie believe they have seen the monster. There the orchestra builds towards a climax, but instead of the expected rhythm, Pentland achieves her dramatic moment by leaving the orchestra silent.

5.11 *The Lake*, bars 241–247. See p. 62.

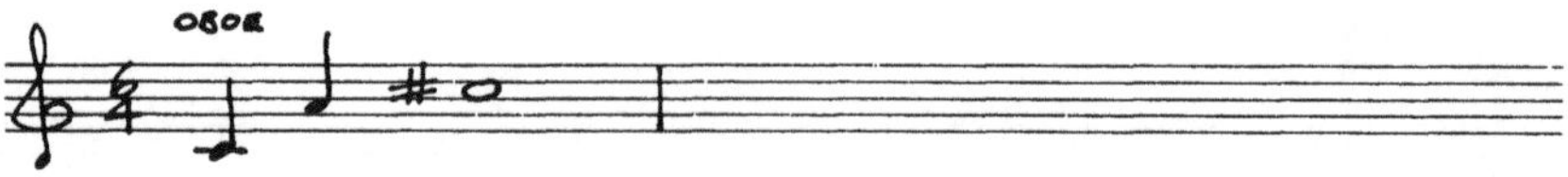

5.12 *The Lake*, bar 3, oboe. See p. 63.

5.13 *The Lake*, 2nd section, bars 1–3, flute. See p. 63.

5.14 *The Lake*, bars 197–198, piano only. See p. 63.

As in most of the other works of her mature style, Pentland does not use set melodies. The melodic passages are made from a constant reassembly of a few short rhythms and melodic intervals. The principal intervals are a ninth and seventh, both major and minor (sometimes presented as augmented and diminished octaves), a fourth, and a sixth. The ninths and sevenths are often presented in three-note groups with a third between the outside notes of the interval (as in Examples 5.12 and 5.13). Example 5.14 shows both the melodic and harmonic use of these motifs – melodically in the treble part of the piano, and harmonically between treble and bass on beats 2 and 4.

The vocal parts make use of the same melodic motifs but are governed more by a slight exaggeration of the natural speech rhythm. Pentland also uses *Sprechstimme* (speech-song) for the vocal parts, a technique used by Schoenberg most effectively in his *Pierrot Lunaire* (1912), in which the voice part is spoken on a pitch approximating that written. In *The Lake, Sprechstimme* and the natural speech rhythms give the vocal parts more a rhythmic than a melodic flavour. The work is most successful in its broad dramatic aspects, and the composer has sacrificed vocal and instrumental lyricism for this goal.

The frequent use of the monster leitmotif and other easily recognized motifs can be considered to be a part of Pentland's attempt to write on the broadest level. She has also written much fine detail which surfaces only after some familiarity with the work. The rather intricate way she has assembled the interval motifs, both harmonically and melodically, makes it appear initially that she has used a wide assortment of materials. But there are only a few motivic ingredients and she has cleverly varied them to create the overall dramatic impression needed. She has chosen wisely, for if the detail were obvious it would call attention to itself and detract from the drama.

The Lake is not a demanding work technically because of the limitations imposed by the commission. The tenor part is fairly simple, as are most of the instrumental parts, and, in keeping with the original request, the entire work takes slightly under half an hour to perform. Unfortunately, the London ensemble lost interest in the composition before seeing it, and the opera was not performed until 1954, when it was presented as a radio program on 'CBC Wednesday Night.' In a review for the *Canadian Forum* (Apr 1954) Milton Wilson noticed some resemblance to Copland's writing. He was enthusiastic about the composition and recommended that it deserved 'to be taken up by theatrical groups for stage performance.' The small ensemble required and the relatively untaxing demands on the performers recommend this work to amateur groups interested in a modern chamber opera.

The fact that the reviewer was reminded of Copland suggests that even at this stage of her transition Pentland's style still held some strong elements of her past. In this case the element referred to was short and austere melodic phrases, soemthing she had adopted in the mid-1940s as a permanent part of her style. But in the harmonic and rhythmic setting of *The Lake* she had not separated her writing from that of her teacher as much as she had thought. Later, when the transition to serial technique was complete, the same kind of phrases would no longer remind a listener of Copland.

In an article for *Northern Review* in 1950, Pentland looked back over the previous twenty years of Canadian music and remarked on the changes. She was pleased to note that 'creative music is becoming part of the university curriculum, and Handel is finally dethroned as the model for the composition students,' and she praised the slow but steady increase in the willingness of performers and audiences to give new compositions a hearing. We can see a change of attitude about which twentieth-century influences were important in her statement that 'there are the few [Canadian composers], fortunately, who have evolved with the music of our time, taking as their natural heritage the great trends of the century inherent in the work of Schoenberg, Bartok, Stravinsky, Hindemith.' In her new list only Hindemith and Stravinsky retain their position from her article of seven years earlier. Copland is not mentioned, but in his place is Bartók, who also used short, incisive rhythmic motifs and national themes; and Schoenberg, who had once been mentioned with qualifications, now heads the list. The statement clearly reflects her new goals – a union of the harmonic practices of Schoenberg and Hindemith with the type of rhythmic drive found in Bartók and Stravinsky.

In the light of her outspoken antagonism towards backward-looking composers, it is easy to imagine her outrage over the description of her music in a 1950 article in *Canadian Writing*. The writer, Rudolph Kestler, had inexplicably confused her with another composer and described her works as lyrical along the lines of Fauré and Richard Strauss. He cites as an example of her writing *Woodland Sketches*, compositions by Edward MacDowell (1861–1908). In an angry letter to the editor she affirms the right of a critic to pan any work he disagrees with, but not totally to distort the facts. 'Most of my previous detractors

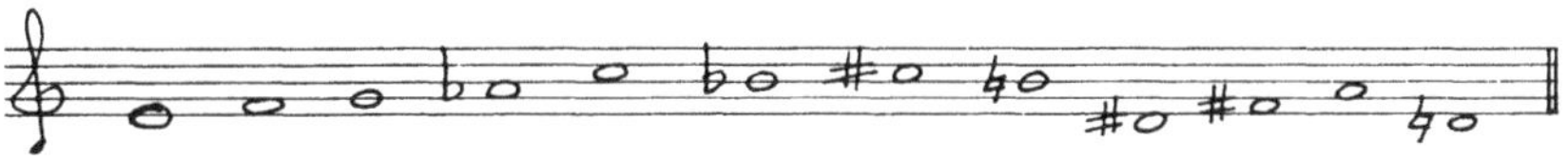

5.15 *String Quartet No. 2*, basic series. See p. 65.

55
tr
60
pp
sul tasto
sul tasto
pp
sul tasto
sul tasto

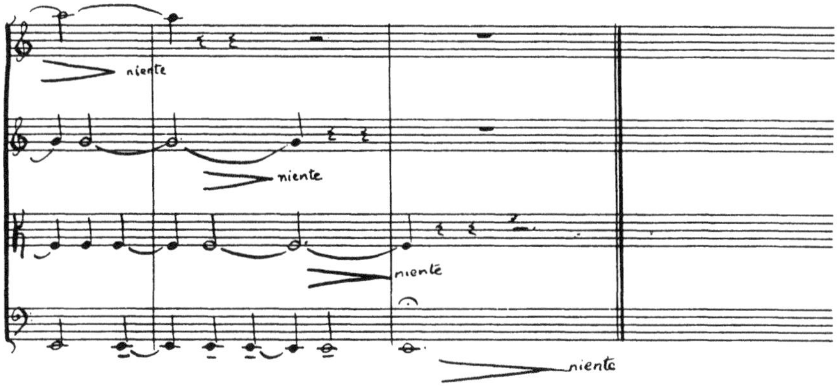

5.16 *String Quartet No. 2*, 1st movement, bars 1–11, 56–62. See p. 66.

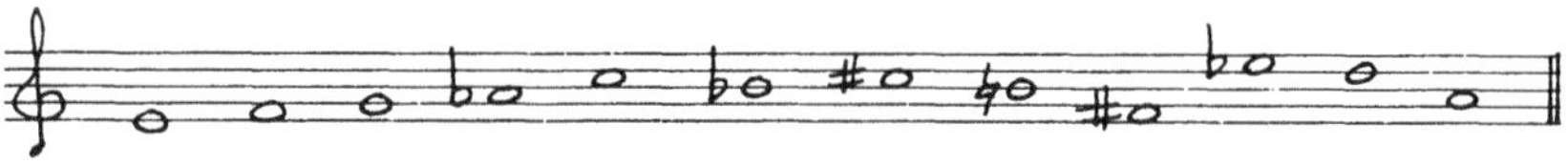

5.17 *String Quartet No. 2*, basic series, 5th movement, bars 9 and 10. See p. 65.

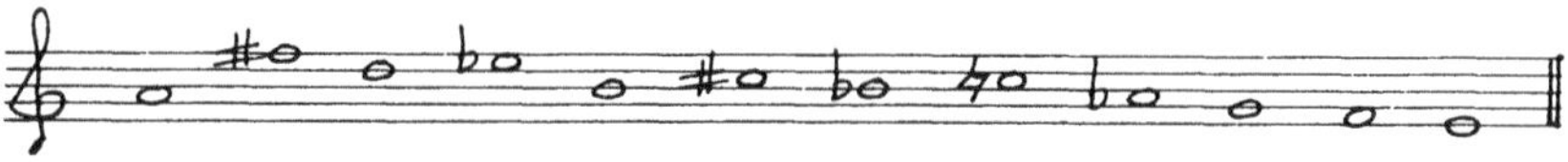

5.18 *String Quartet No. 2*, basic series, 5th movement, end. See p. 65.

5.19 *String Quartet No. 2*, motto theme. See p. 65.

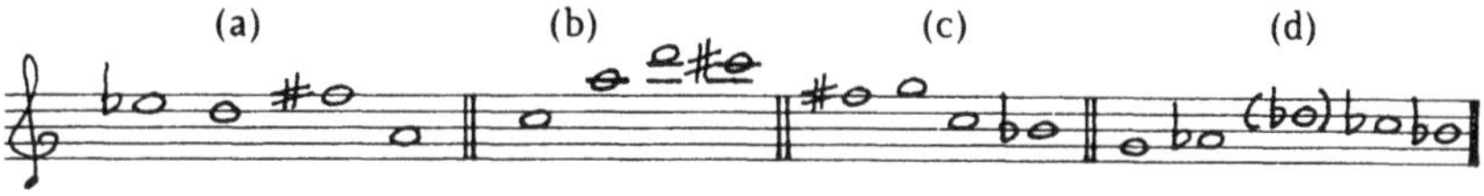

5.20 *String Quartet No. 2*, variants of last 4 notes: (a) 1st movement; (b) 2nd movement; (c) 3rd movement; (d) 4th movement. See p. 66.

5.21 *String Quartet No. 2*, 5th movement, bars 1–5, 148–156. See p. 66.

would have been very happy to have found traces of Fauré and/or R. Strauss in my works, but never, alas, in all my thirty years of composing, even in my student days, could I oblige them in this fashion.'

After completion of *The Lake*, *String Quartet No. 2* occupied most of Pentland's creative efforts until November 1953, interrupted only for the short time it took to compose *Two-Piano Sonata*. The amount of time spent on *Quartet No. 2* – more than a year – is exceptional for this period and indicates the effort she was concentrating on the incorporation of the elements of serial technique into her writing. In *String Quartet No. 2* we can find some of her best neo-classic formal structures as well as the first evidence of what could be considered a closely serial composition. The structure of each movement is controlled with the same attention to tiny detail found earlier in *Sonata Fantasy*; and the five movements are carefully related in a way Pentland had not attempted before. In this work she has found the solution to her search for unification of her neo-classic techniques with the major elements of serialization.

Each movement sounds different from all the others, and indeed the composer has taken pains to make that impression. The five separate formal structures, each with its own rhythmic-melodic motifs, texture, and mood, have substantial independence from one another on the level of musical communication. They are united, however, on a far less obvious level in that they have in common a single tone row and, just as important in Pentland's technique of composition, several characteristic intervals that are derived from the common row. The fine details of this technical interrelationship would require a lengthy essay to expose, so intricate are they. But a simple overview will give an idea of the composer's approach and suggest directions for a more detailed technical analysis.

The basic series used in the work is shown in Example 5.15, and it appears in this form at the beginning of the first movement (see Example 5.16). It is found also in bars 9 and 10 of the fifth movement with a variant of the last four notes (Example 5.17), and in retrograde, with another variant of the same notes (Example 5.18), at the end of the last movement. The other three movements use variations of the row that are not as easily identified. But no matter what the full variant is, in each movement Pentland works with the elements of what she has called a 'motto theme' (see Example 5.19).

The motto, in its original form, consists of two half-step intervals separated by a full step, and it is this rather innocent-looking set of intervals that is used in each movement as both an important unifying device and one of the major sources of melodic material. There is one additional motivic element also taken from the row – the intervals of the last four notes which are different in each of the row variants but always include a half-step as an essential element (some of the various mutations can be seen in Example 5.20).

All the recurring motifs in *String Quartet No.* 2, no matter what their variation, contain a half-step, and the connection between the movements can actually be heard on that level: there is always a half-step in the melodic motifs. The other audible unifying device is the use of the same kind of opening passage in the first and last movements: the entrances of the four instruments successively on the notes E, F, G, A flat (the motto theme), and the reverse of the entrance bars at the end of both those movements. Because the beginnings and ends of the first and fifth movements are the reverse of one another, i.e. low note first and last in the first movement and high note first and last in the fifth movement, they take on the outward appearance of the mirror of each other. (Compare Example 5.16 with Example 5.21.)

The technical organization of a work is, of course, not its musical essence but only its mechanical basis. On the level of musical organization each movement of the quartet maintains an individual identity, and for all their technical similarities, the first and fifth movements are musically quite different.

The first movement begins with a slow and definite pace, building constantly from a very soft entrance, but never hurried. (See Example 5.16.) A four-note rhythmic motif, ♪♩♪ ♩., grows finally from the opening two-note short–long rhythms, and the remainder of the movement is an intense development of both this motif and the plodding opening rhythm. Until the movement fades out at the end (Example 5.21), it never loses its aura of methodical intensity.

Using the same basic tonal, intervallic, and rhythmic motifs, Pentland creates a very different mood in the fifth movement. By using a faster tempo, ♩ = 100 (♩ = 60 in the first movement), and pulsing accents on the short–long rhythm, the fifth movement begins with a frantic, almost belligerent mood. It is only in the final bars, when the plodding rhythm from the first movement is restated, that the movement calms down and brings the quartet to a close with a section that melodically and harmonically mirrors the beginning and emotionally brings it to rest.

The motto also plays an important harmonic role in the composition. The basic harmonic sound of the composition is tied to the intervals of

5.22 *String Quartet No. 2*, 2nd movement, bars 7–10, 80–82. See p. 67.

5.23 *String Quartet No. 2*, 3rd movement, bars 33–36. See p. 67.

5.24 *String Quartet No. 2*, 4th movement, bars 1–7. See p. 67.

the motto. In the first movement, by the simple device of keeping each instrument on its opening pitch, the intervals of the motto become the first full harmony heard (see Example 5.16), and these intervals are found at important structural places throughout each movement, as for example the last chord of Example 5.22.

For the second movement Pentland has chosen an energetic variation of the short-long rhythmic motif that is reminiscent of the fourth movement of *Symphony No. 2*. (Compare Example 5.9 with Example 5.22.) There is a musical quotation from the chant of the requiem mass included between bars 128 and 140 of this movement. The rhythm fits in easily – it is a version of the plodding rhythm – and it is worked in as a personal reference rather than something for the listener to pick out. The entire quartet is dedicated to the memory of her brother Charles, who died in an airplane crash in March 1953.

The third movement is a rustic dance which uses the short–long rhythm in a more relaxed and whimsical manner (Example 5.23), and the fourth movement is a fugue in the irregular metre of 7/8, which carries a more detached character (see Example 5.24).

String Quartet No. 2 exhibits both variety and unity. The five movements share a common fund of technical source material but present widely different moods. The movements complement one another by a contrast of mood and tempo and present a total impression of a single musical idea. The quartet is not easy listening and was not intended to be. It is deeply introspective and skilfully assembled and rewards the listener who would spend the time and effort necessary to become acquainted with it. It ranks with the very best of Pentland's compositions.

The years of transition were very productive for Pentland and quite successful in terms of performances both in Canada and elsewhere. *String Quartet No. 1* had its première in Philadelphia in a concert of 'Chamber Music by Women of 5 Countries' in 1949 and was played again in 1950 at the Vancouver Symposium of Canadian Contemporary Music, a highly successful showcase for Canadian talent that drew a total audience of 5,000. In 1953 Pentland performed four of her own compositions, *Variations for Piano*, *Sonata Fantasy*, *Dirge* (1948), and *Sonatina No. 2* (1951), on a program of 'Works of Northwest Composers' in Seattle, Washington. The two Seattle newspaper critics gave negative reviews of the programmed works, but both praised her encore, *Studies in Line*. *Piano Sonata* was performed in Prague; the CBC and BBC broadcast several of her works; and Harry Adaskin continued to play her compositions – in 1949 he performed *Vista* (1945) in Wisconsin, Montreal, and Toronto.

The critics supplied a variety of reactions to her music – often negative, but occasionally positive and sometimes even perceptive. *Ave atque vale* (1951), for example, drew mixed reviews on its première by the Vancouver Symphony in 1953. Stanley Bligh of the *Sun* pointed out 'the skilful use of color contrasts and utilization of the resources of the orchestra,' but refrained from making a judgment by acknowledging that 'to appraise a new work on first hearing is an exceedingly difficult task.' The *Province* critic, Ida Halpern, did not hesitate: 'We found as yet no definite style of her own in Miss Pentland's composition but a strong leaning toward Shostakovich.' Her final comment was a rephrase of a condescending remark she had made in several earlier reviews: 'It is highly commendable to give hearings to such serious music-writers and Miss Pentland, still young, could in time develop the expression of her own individuality.' Pentland had received backhanded praise like this before, but it still must have been somewhat painful at forty-one, with her background, to receive the kind of remark usually reserved for an inexperienced composer. None the less, whatever she thought of Shostakovich, he was at least a more contemporary composer than Fauré, Strauss, and MacDowell!

Along with the jabs of the bland and negative reviews came a number of encouraging reactions from other critics and audiences. The years in Vancouver had been overwhelmingly positive; she had noted in the 1950 article that 'the western provinces may perhaps present less hostility to new ideas.' She was happy teaching at the University of British Columbia and found time to turn out a great variety of compositions: several works for string orchestra and full orchestra, a string quartet, a chamber opera, a woodwind octet, choral music, and solo compositions for violin, flute, and piano.

No sooner had she reconciled the old and new techniques in *String Quartet No. 2* than a series of new influences changed her direction again. The second big change in Pentland's technique was the total abandonment of the Hindemith-Copland techniques in favour of her personal version of the serial technique, but with some new basic ideas held over from developments during the transition period. It all came about quite unplanned as the result of a trip to Europe.

6

Second style Part I 1955–1958

As a result of a BBC broadcast of her *Symphony No. 2*, Pentland had been invited to perform a program of her own music for the Professional Women's Club of Brussels in the summer of 1955. She had not been back to Europe since her student days with Gauthiez and the invitation was a good excuse to take a break. The previous six years of teaching, composing, and performing had been intensive and a change of scene seemed a good idea. In addition to the Brussels performance she arranged a concert and a BBC recording session in London and planned to attend some music festivals to hear the latest developments in European music.

Once again her summer vacation provided the source for new approaches to composition – this time a crystalization of the new techniques she was using. The summer festival circuit in Europe was flourishing during the 1950s and Pentland was able to attend several that featured contemporary music. Her first and most important stop was the Darmstadt Internationale Ferienkurse für neue Musik where she heard electronic works by Boulez, Stockhausen, Nono, and Berio and was especially impressed by the music of Anton Webern and that of other composers who took him as their model. The styles, techniques, and experiments suggested new avenues of exploration, and the ten days Pentland spent in Darmstadt provided the raw material she needed for the new directions in her career. She assimilated elements of many of the approaches she heard there, especially those of Webern.

Pentland's first small exposure to the music of Webern had been at the MacDowell Colony in 1947 and 1948, while she was beginning to appreciate the serial technique as used by Schoenberg. In Darmstadt she found Webern's music even more attractive. Webern's style is one of extreme economy in which each pitch, each rhythm, and each tone colour are weighted with infinite care, and this had a profound effect on Pentland; she wrote in *Music Scene* (July–Aug. 1968): 'I realized you can say as much with two notes as with twenty if you use the right two in the right place'(9). This was to be the basis of her new style. If her works written before 1955 can be described as spare, direct, linear, and controlled, those written afterwards are even more so. Since 1947 she had slowly eliminated from her writing many of the elements she had begun to think of as 'superfluous busy-ness,' such as octave doublings and scale passages. In the music of Webern she could see a model for the final step in her change of style: elimination of all non-essential notes, making the music extremely transparent. She put the theory into practice immediately, and her compositions written shortly after the trip already show her conscious effort to be more economical in her writing, as for example in *Interlude* (1955), *Concerto for Piano and Strings* (1955–6), and especially in *Symphony for Ten Parts* (No. 3) (1957).

In *Symphony for Ten Parts* (her third symphony) she achieved a new level of economy, transparency, and contrast – the essential musical elements of her second style. The three movements display three different applications of the new technique. The basic approach can be seen in the opening bars of the first movement (Example 6.1), which exhibit a high degree of sensitivity to the minute points of colour, shading, and blend, characteristics that immediately associate this composition with the approach of Webern. In the first three bars there are fewer notes but far more information than in past compositions. The Webern technique can be seen in isolated notes introduced by a single instrument; the mixing of contrasting tone colours (xylophone, plucked string, bowed string, trumpet); detailed marking of each note for volume, exact articulation, and tone shading; and complex rhythm.

The thematic elements from which the movement is built are the intervals of the first four notes, and the rhythm of a triplet, seen in its most condensed form in the xylophone part of bar 3. The entire movement proceeds as a working-out and elaboration of these elements, a multi-faceted development of the two motifs, including techniques not seen before in Pentland's music. Throughout the movement the melodic and rhythmic motifs are elaborated by contrasts of instrumental colour, varieties of texture, and contrasts of volume, range, and articulation. The overall effect is one of extreme variety in all possible

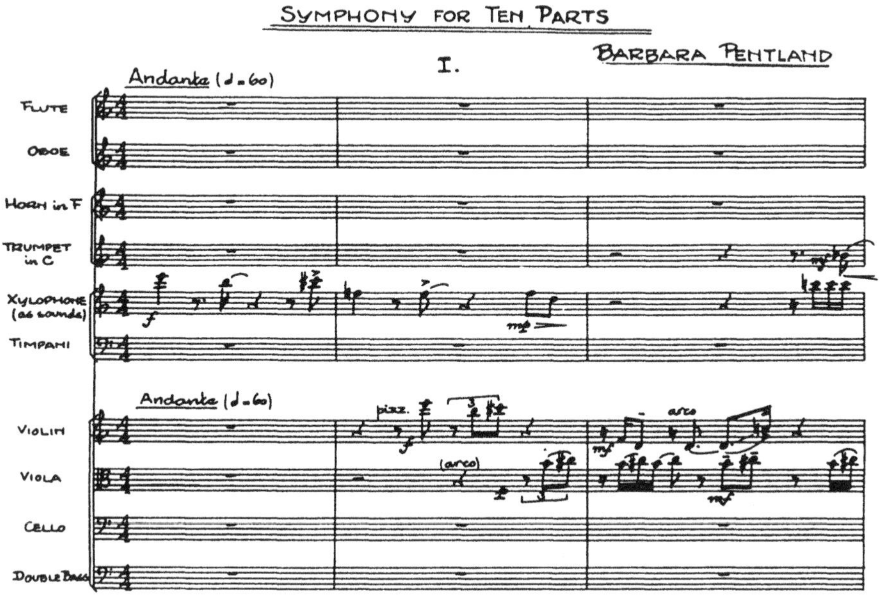

6.1 *Symphony for Ten Parts*, 1st movement, bars 1–3. See p. 70.

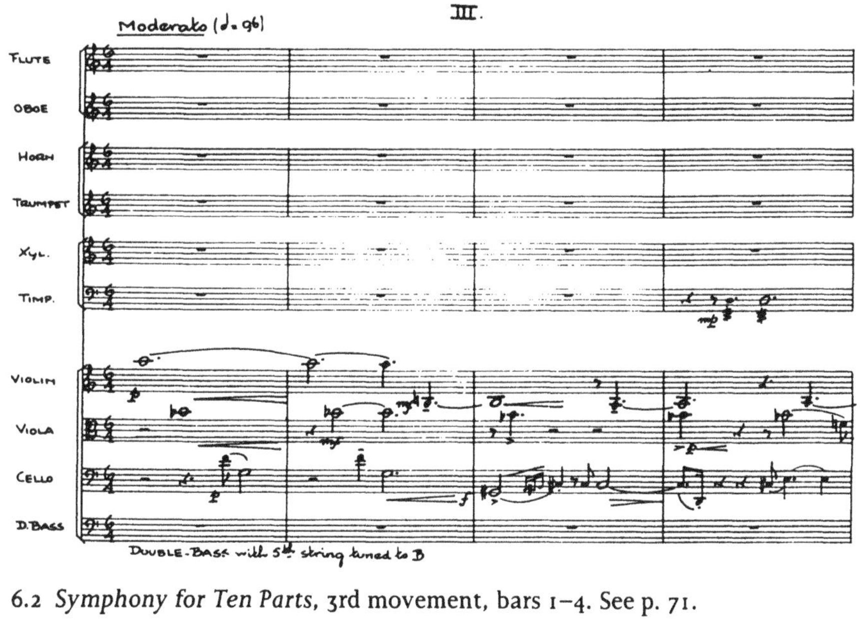

6.2 *Symphony for Ten Parts*, 3rd movement, bars 1–4. See p. 71.

6.3 *Symphony for Ten Parts*, 3rd movement, bars 17–22. See p. 71.

musical elements – colour, rhythm, and texture – presenting a pointillistic array of sound, all from a small source introduced in miniature in the first several bars.

In the third movement the same sensitivity to detail is exhibited, but in a different way. Instead of the rapid and somewhat disjointed change of colour, here the opening pace is more gradual, and the listener's attention is directed to the blend and contrast of the shades of dynamics, to the slight variation in note stress, and to small changes in the distance of the entries. (See Example 6.2.) The beginning of this movement is based on a 'threeness,' i.e. three successive entries and the contrast of a cluster of three sustained pitches in different octaves. No new material is introduced from bar 1 to bar 2 – the notes remain virtually the same – but there are new dynamics, new relationships of volume, new emphasis in the cello part, and a shortening of the space between the entrances. The change of the status of the cello note F, from quasi-grace note in bar 1 to a definite member of the tonal contrast in bar 2, is a good example of the economy of statement on which this movement relies.

Throughout the symphony Pentland economizes by allowing small changes in the assembly of notes and rhythms to carry the work forward. One must pay close attention to very small changes in rhythm, tone colour, or balance. Pentland has learned not to hammer her points at the listeners but to require them to concentrate on changes of a much more delicate nature. Everything happens in miniature, and the total performance takes only ten minutes. Just as important to her new concept of presentation is her awareness of the use of variety in pace and texture. She has totally abandoned her Baroque-like steadiness, and the result is a composition that jumps forward and stands still for irregular lengths of time, with rapid changes in the number of moving voices from one moment to the next. In this symphony she has rethought each element.

Even the make-up of the ensemble of the symphony is reminiscent of the Webern style in that there is no massive ensemble required; it is a chamber ensemble with one player on a part: flute, oboe, horn, trumpet, xylophone, timpani, and one each of the four strings. The timpani at times is treated more as a melody instrument than in its more traditional use for punctuation or heightening of loud passages (see Example 6.3).

Symphony for Ten Parts is tightly composed and unified by elements that more and more were to become a part of Pentland's technique. She has drawn the principal melodic material of each movement from the same source. Each movement opens with the same two intervals, although the actual groupings are different:

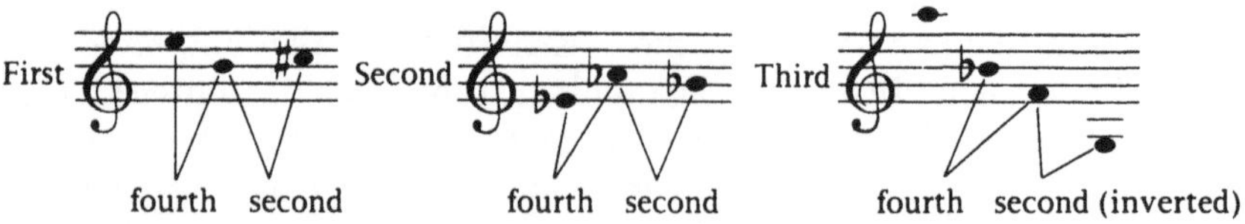

In addition, the entire work is given a sense of cyclic construction by the device of recalling the beginning of the first movement in the very last bars of the last movement, where the original form of the common motif E, B, C sharp is used (compare Examples 6.4 and 6.1), and the symphony ends as it began, with the xylophone.

As if to emphasize the symmetry of the beginning and ending bars the middle movement has within it a complete mirror: the last forty bars (84–123) are an exact mirror of the first forty (see Example 6.5) and the middle forty-four bars are given over to development of the thematic material. Mirror is a device used by composers from as early as the fifteenth century, and was utilized by the Viennese school (Schoenberg, Berg, Webern) as a method of unifying some of their twelve-tone compositions. Webern's *Chamber Symphony*, op 21 (1928), for example, makes extensive use of mirror as a structural device. It is a logical tool for a compositional technique that involves numbers and close attention to the fine points of transparent construction. Another and perhaps a natural result of the constant association of serial composers with numbers is that they often become interested to some extent in numerology (Schoenberg was virtually possessed by it). Pentland's involvement with this aspect of the technique was not very serious, but some attention to numbers can be seen in the construction of the opening sections of all three movements of the symphony: in the initial statements of the themes, the first movement requires a single instrument, the second requires two instruments, and third three instruments. In a work so closely tied to Webern-Schoenberg ideas, this would not appear to be an accident. (The only other numerological association found in her writing occurs in *Diasters of the Sun* in which there are seven movements and seven major motifs. See chapter 7.)

As much as she borrowed the techniques and devices of the Viennese school, even at this point in her career Pentland did not follow their strict observation of the twelve-tone row. The row technique, in which

6.4 *Symphony for Ten Parts*, 3rd movement, last three bars. See p. 72.

6.5 *Symphony for Ten Parts*, 2nd movement, bars 1–5, 119–123. See p. 72.

no note is used out of numerical order, was developed in order to help avoid a promise of tonality when none was intended. Pentland often begins her works with a row or part of a row, but for her, serial technique is more of a principle rather than a series of strict laws to be obeyed throughout each work. In the symphony, as in many other works to be discussed, it is possible to find all or part of a row at the beginning of a movement, but Pentland abandons her row easily. What she wanted was the impression a row gives – that of non-tonality and a high degree of equality among the twelve notes of the scale, but she found that it was not necessary to adhere strictly to the Schoenberg system in order to achieve that goal. In the symphony, instead of presenting the entire row in the opening measures of each movement, she brings it out gradually with repeats of individual notes (Example 6.1, bar 2), or entire phrases (bars 2 and 3, viola).

Symphony for Ten Parts, for all of its use of Viennese techniques and Webern's economy, is still very much a composition of Pentland. Her particular brand of direct and spare melody coupled with lively rhythms is present even with the new techniques. Each movement contains a separate mood and, although the opening sounds of the first movement are recalled at the very end of the last movement, the moods are not similar. The first movement introduces irregular rhythmic motion, fine details of colour, and rapid changes of texture. These elements are combined with dramatic outbursts that punctuate the irregular flow of the phrases and give to the entire movement great energy and colour.

The second movement is a whimsical working-out of the first three-note rhythm and melodic shape. The perky staccato notes, the constant jumping from instrument to instrument, and unexpected halts in the forward motion produce a very light mood.

For complete contrast the composer presents her heaviest material in the last movement. The staggered entrance of the instruments and the angular motion with sustained and overlapping tone clusters express a tortured and anguished mood. The intensity of this movement is a result of the development of the basic opposition of adjacent tones built into the first bar: the harmonic opposition of A and B flat, of B flat and G, and of A, B flat and G, and the melodic opposition of F and G (in the cello). (See Example 6.2.) Throughout the movement both the technical content and emotional tension of that first bar is continued without relaxation, and it is only in the last bars, where the mirror of material from the first movement is introduced, that the association of all movements is clearly brought out when the common three-note group is finally brought back in its original shape. Pentland has combined Webern's techniques with her own ideas of sound, mood, and energy.

After the festival at Darmstadt, Pentland went on to Brussels for the concerts of her works, which included a première of her *Solo Violin Sonata* (1950), performed by Louis Thienpont, *Sonata for Cello and Piano* (1943), played by Antoinette Dethoor and Marcelle Vandemoortel, and several piano compositions, including *Sonata Fantasy* (1947), *Dirge* (1948), *Sonatina No. 1* and *Sonatina No. 2* (both 1951), and *Aria* (1954), all performed by the composer.

From Brussels she journeyed to Baden-Baden for the 1955 Festival of the International Society for Contemporary Music (ISCM), where she represented the Canadian League of Composers. At this prestigious festival selected works from all over the world are performed for an élite audience of composers and performers. The Canadian League of Composers had submitted seven works, including Pentland's *String Quartet No. 2*, to the festival committee for consideration that year, but the scores arrived after the jury deadline and therefore no Canadian works were chosen.

The highlight of the festival was the first performance of Pierre Boulez's *Le Marteau sans maître* (1954, revised 1957), a group of vocal settings with instrumental 'commentaries.' The work was important to Pentland because it is not strictly serial while maintaining its non-tonal character, a technique she was already using, and also because it deals with density, colour, and sound contrasts, elements she had not yet explored in detail. It would seem that this was the other big influence on *Symphony for Ten Parts*. From Webern she took the ideas of miniature, delicate nuance, and subtle contrast, and from Boulez the changes of density and sound contrast, and the realization that all of these elements could work outside the framework of strict serialism. She distilled the essence from these techniques and created music that was exclusively her own. 'I am not a slave to [any] system nor [a] follower of methods of others. A creative mind can only use material through inner transformation.' Webern, Boulez, and others had provided the basic techniques that Pentland then synthesized and used to her own ends through 'inner transformation,' i.e. by understanding the purpose and energy of the technique and adapting it to her own style.

The last stop on the summer tour was London, where the BBC had made arrangements to record some of Pentland's piano works for broadcast. The program included *Variations for Piano*, *Piano Sonata*, the two sonatinas, *Studies in Line*, *Dirge*, and *Sonata Fantasy*, which she recorded the day after presenting them in live performance at St Cecilia's House under the auspices of the Institute of Contemporary Arts.

The summer of 1955 had been full and enlightening. Pentland had been exposed to some exciting new influences which would help her develop her own compositions, and the trip had given her the opportunity to present herself as a composer and performer in Europe. She returned to Vancouver to teach at the university for another year but by the time she arrived in Canada she was already making plans to return to the continent for a longer stay.

Interlude was completed by the end of the summer, and during the school year, in addition to her teaching obligations, she started *Concerto for Piano and Strings*. When summer arrived she was off to Europe again; this time for a full year of listening and composing.

Pentland returned to the summer course at Darmstadt where she continued to work on the concerto. From there she travelled to Salzburg for the Unesco conference on opera in radio, television, and film and then on to Venice for the Festival Internazionale di Musica Contemporanea and the world première of Stravinsky's *Canticum sacrum* at St Mark's Basilica. The event was popular and Pentland was lucky enough to get inside the basilica with a press pass secured by a friend, while much of the audience remained outside in the piazza where they listened through loudspeakers.

The 1956 ISCM Festival was held in Stockholm, and this time Pentland attended as a participant. Her *String Quartet No. 2*, which had been submitted too late for the 1955 festival, had been selected for performance. It was one of the 27 chosen from a field of 140 entries and was the second Canadian work ever selected (in 1954 a work by Jean Coulthard had been performed). But just as the festival began, serious complications threatened to block performance of Pentland's piece.

The Canadian League of Composers had been in existence only since 1951 and was very proud to have a composition by one of its members singled out for international acclaim. The organization, however, had very limited funds, and when the Swedish section of the ISCM notified it that it would be charged $160 for the musicians to play Pentland's composition, it was faced with an unexpected financial crisis. The league officers in Toronto were summoned by president John Weinzweig to an emergency meeting. The league's finances were so meagre that it had not yet paid the ISCM yearly membership fee of $120 for the preceding year, and the added performance expense caused the officers to weigh seriously the benefits of the affiliation. After much discussion they decided to resign from the ISCM and withdraw the entry (Pentland's quartet), in order to spend their meagre treasury on performances in Canada; they immediately informed both the ISCM directorate (in Stockholm) and Pentland of their decision.

The ISCM replied by accepting with regret the resignation of the Canadian group, but stating that the program for the 1956 festival was set and that the Pentland quartet would go on as scheduled. Karl-Birger Blomdahl, secretary of the ISCM, secured an offer from Swedish Radio to finance the performance by a Swedish quartet for later broadcast, and finally the president of the University of British Columbia arranged to support the performance with university funds. The quartet was well received and Pentland was encouraged by the favourable remarks of a number of the distinguished participants. As usual, however, not everyone was pleased; a Swedish newspaper critic reported that 'Miss Pentland was very attractive but her music was not' – a remark that was picked up by the Montreal press.

The resignation of the Canadian League of Composers was certainly ill-timed from Pentland's standpoint, and in her isolation in Vancouver from the decision-making executive in Toronto she felt victimized. The event ultimately turned out well for her, but she harboured ill feelings towards the Torontonians for years afterwards.

The summer festivals were a fine experience, but Pentland's goal that year (1956–7) was to live for a period of time in an active musical centre where she could hear quality performances of contemporary music. The city she chose was Munich, which provided many of the stimuli she had hoped for. She was especially pleased with the bi-monthly concerts given by the Studio für neue Musik, and for enjoyment of a more relaxed nature she had the friendship of Marion and Anna-Maria (Amsel) Bembé, daughters of the widow from whom she rented a room. Marion was just beginning a career as a painter – one of her works hangs in Pentland's studio in Vancouver – and Amsel was a piano student of Gertrude Hindemith (wife of the composer). Pentland and Amsel whiled away many hours playing two-piano works even though the pianos were in separate rooms across the hall! The Bembé household was a pleasant place for work, and it was there that she completed both *Concerto for Piano and Strings* and *Symphony for Ten Parts* and began *Toccata*.

Although written just before the symphony, *Concerto for Piano and*

6.6 *Concerto for Piano and Strings*, 1st movement, bars 1–10. See p. 77.

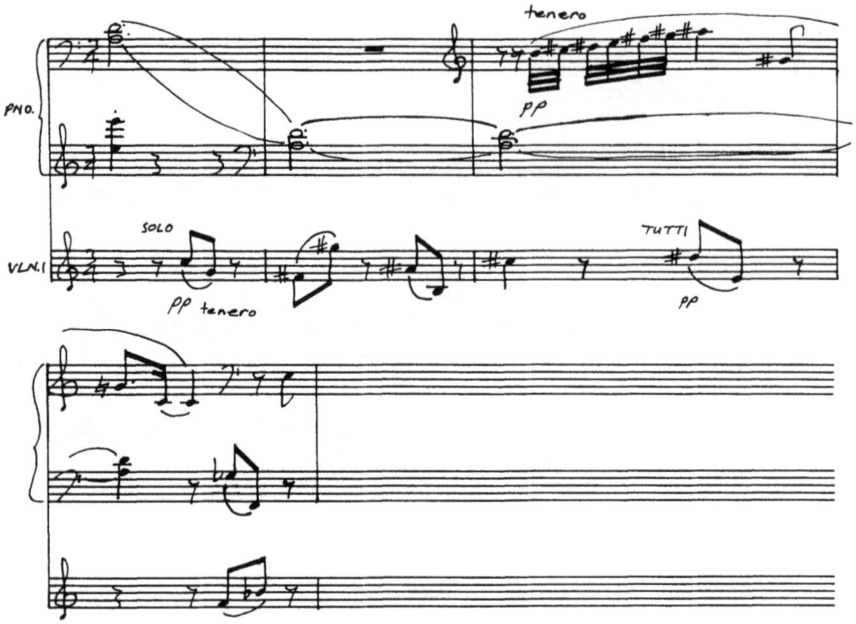

6.7 *Concerto for Piano and Strings*, 1st movement, bars 36–39. See p. 77.

6.8 *Concerto for Piano and Strings*, 1st movement, bars 1–5. See p. 78.

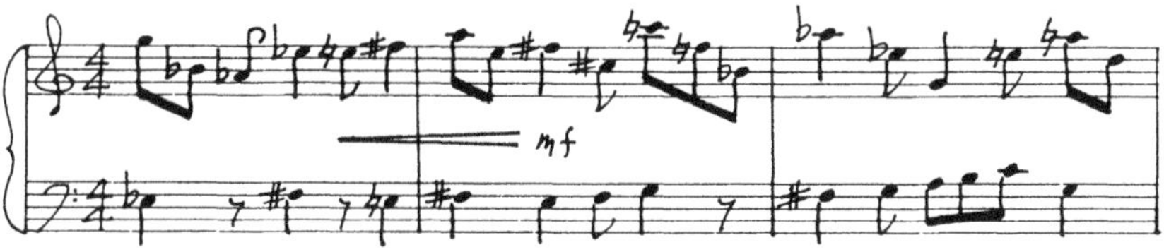

6.9 *Concerto for Piano and Strings*, 3rd movement, bars 23–25, piano. See p. 78.

6.9 *Concerto for Piano and Strings*, 3rd movement, bars 99–103. See p. 78.

6.9 *Concerto for Piano and Strings*, 3rd movement, bars 152–154. See p. 78.

Strings uses a somewhat different approach. In general, it lies midway between the pre-Darmstadt style and the new style found in the symphony. Throughout her career Pentland has used the opening statement as the source of all the material for a movement (her term for it is 'initial impulse'), and this basic approach can be found in nearly all her compositions. After 1955, changes can be seen in the kinds of 'initial impulse' chosen and in the economy of both the first statement and its working-out. In these terms the concerto can be viewed as a mid-point; not as prolix as, say, *String Quartet No. 2*, but not as terse as the symphony and successive works. The new ideas can be seen in the length and nature of the opening statement, the constant change of pace throughout each movement, and the tendency towards transparent orchestration which she achieves by writing for fewer instruments at any one time and avoiding duplication of lines.

The first movement of the concerto has two basic motifs, introduced by the solo piano in the first four bars of the composition (see Example 6.6). The first motif is composed of two notes in an accented, uneven rhythm (♪♩ or ♫); the second is a figure of four even notes (♬♬). In the opening statement, motif 2 actually grows from motif 1 (bar 4) although at that point the two motifs are combined in a single phrase with a single energetic mood. It is only after the opening statement that the two motifs take on contrasting characters.

When separated, the first motif continues with the opening mood of energetic impatience while the second motif becomes more relaxed and lyrical. As the movement progresses the motifs grow into longer phrases and are expanded individually and combined; at various points one motif is given the character of the other, for example, at bar 36 where the energetic motif 1 is given the subdued, relaxed and lyrical attitude of the second motif (see Example 6.7). The overall attitude of the movement is somewhat light-hearted and full of energy for the most part, but there are occasional sections of a more pensive mood. Of the three movements, the first contains the largest amount of new influences in its constant and unpredictable changes of pace and economy of expression. The second movement has some of these qualities, but for the most part the denseness of the writing and the expansiveness of the opening theme remind one more of the earlier works. The third movement, too, suggests an earlier influence in its Coplandesque theme and working-out. (Copland was present for the première of the concerto but apparently took no notice of the similarities – at least he never mentioned them to Pentland.)

The third movement is based on a one-bar melody that alternates with a regular, drone-like accompaniment and presents a bouncy, folkish mood. Even the harmony suggests the older influence; the slow pace at which the twelve-tone row is introduced would suggest at first that the harmonic organization was that of the older intervallic one rather than the new serial technique (see Example 6.8). The movement is in a clearly audible rondo form that exudes fun and good humour through a clever manipulation of its rhythmic organization, such as the changes in Example 6.9.

Taken as a whole, *Concerto for Piano and Strings* is a bright and energetic work. The two contrasting moods found in the first movement are individually explored in the second and third: the lyrical and pensive aspect is developed in the second movement, and the rhythmic, lighter mood in the third.

One can see in the concerto and in the symphony that Pentland's new style was more than just the use of serial technique as a basic element of harmonic and melodic control. There were other new ideas as well: the compositions written after 1955 have shorter and sharper melodic-rhythmic motifs which are more flexible, and the works are therefore less dense in terms of numbers of notes per bar; the orchestration is much thinner; and the individual movements contain a number of changes of pace. By the time Pentland began consciously to adopt these new elements into her style, all but one, change of pace, could already be seen to some degree in her compositions. But to change the pace of a single movement, that is, the texture and the rate at which new information is presented, was very difficult for Pentland. Beginning in her Juilliard days with Jacobi she had learned to keep the pace constant in imitation of the Renaissance masters; variety was to be achieved through other means. The new style, however, not merely allowed pace change but even demanded it, and this has become an element she has continued to develop since the mid-1950s. It is perhaps the most noticeable new element in the new style.

The shorter motifs and thinning out of texture and orchestration had been tendencies since the late 1940s. The difference between the motifs used in *Symphony for Ten Parts* and *Concerto for Piano and Strings* and those, say, of *Symphony No. 2* or *String Quartet No. 2* is mainly one of degree. All the works use motifs; but under the influence of the new European compositions, especially those of Boulez and Webern, Pentland learned to 'put an edge on them,' to select very short motifs that had distinctive rhythms and melodic shapes. In this way she could accomplish in three or four notes what she had formerly done in much longer motivic sections; compare for example the short initial motifs of Examples 6.3 and 6.6 with those of 5.3 and 5.16. The sparser orchestration is a result of the shorter motifs; in order to bring out the subtle changes in the concise new motifs, the scoring had to be made clear. These were the elements she synthesized from listening to the new compositions in Europe, and they fit easily into the new style she had evolved.

Concerto for Piano and Strings had its première in March 1958 at the CBC studios in Toronto, in a concert presented by the Canadian Music Associates, with Mario Bernardi as soloist and Victor Feldbrill conducting the CBC Orchestra. As often happened, her composition brought forth the least charitable remarks from the newspaper reviewers. Hugh Thomson of the *Toronto Star* said he would 'take the gas-pipe and end it all' rather than listen to the work again. Pentland's husband helped to lighten the situation by offering to send Thomson a gas-pipe, and it all seems very funny now; but at the time she was deeply offended. Leslie Bell, writing in the *Star*, stated that the work was 'extremely bad,' which prompted John Beckwith to reply in a letter to Bell, defending the work and questioning Bell's judgment. This gave Bell a second crack which is at least colourfully expressed:

> This concerto appears to be a conscious striving for the nth degree of ugliness.
> In the first movement, the soloist's part consists of tortuous leaps from one end of the keyboard to the other or handfuls of notes clutched from the piano in a vicious, brutal manner. Behind this unpleasant demonstration the strings wander about in a bewildered fashion, finally bringing the movement to an end with a vulgar crunch.
> A lot of the same sort of atmosphere is repeated at a faster tempo in the finale which Miss Pentland's program note is pleased to call 'a rollicking close.' In the second movement, the sound of the strings degenerates into a hideous leer over which the soloist pecks away at the piano in a curious hen-like fashion ... But the ugliness of the Pentland concerto is an ugliness completely divorced of human emotion of any kind. There is no passion; there is no feeling. The work is quite amoral.
> ... The Pentland concerto is 'extremely bad' because it has no soul – because it is so ingenious and clever that it communicates nothing to the listener.

For all the invective it is difficult now to understand what it was that upset the critics. The concerto is attractive and easily understood. It is not lyrical in the Romantic sense, but by 1958 the Toronto public and critics had been exposed to far more harsh sounds than this work. For those already familiar with twentieth-century harmonies, the music can be perceived as full of youthful rhythmic vigour, and the last movement as especially jocular. The composer's own whimsical description sums up the overall impression:

In this Concerto I have tried to use the resources of the piano in a predominantly contrapuntal texture, where the solo is at times pitted independently against the strings and sometimes completely interlocks. Any resemblance to scale passages, traditional or otherwise, is solely intentional, included out of consideration for the performer who may like to feel he still has five or more consecutive fingers on each hand.

Like Life and Ancient Gaul, the concerto is divided into the usual three parts. The first movement, marked Allegro Animato, has contrasting vigorous and tender themes, resembling Youth –, the listener may feel –, but he'll be wrong. It's not supposed to represent anything but the growth of the initial musical impulse. This is projected by the piano at the opening and is the source material for the whole work, as it contains the elements which later fall into the constituent themes. The serial technique is employed as the cohesive means for the various permutations. The slow movement, Largo Tranquillo, may seem as mellow as Middle Age to the listener or may likewise seem to stand still. This is another delusion as, in the guise of continual variation of the basic theme, it's steadily going somewhere even if it circles around and settles down peacefully at the end. But not for long. The Allegro Giocoso bursts in for a Rondo-like finale. Anyone who takes this for Old Age with a twinkle in his eye can certainly have it. In any case, it brings the work to a rollicking close.

In the spring of 1957 Pentland's stay in Munich came to a close. She again attended the ISCM Festival, this time in Zurich, where Schoenberg's opera *Moses und Aron* was given its first stage performance; and from there she travelled to London where Gordon Jeffery performed her *Concerto for Organ and Strings* (1949) at the International Congress of Organists in Westminster Abbey, a performance presented by the Canadian College of Organists. Then she went home once again to Vancouver.

Pentland had barely returned to work in the fall of 1957 when events began that would lead to major changes in her life: marriage and eventual retirement from full-time teaching. In October she was invited to a Sunday afternoon tea party at the home of a friend. It was not the kind of social event that usually interested her (perhaps it was the overtones of the genteel life her mother had planned for her). She turned down the invitation and went to a film that promised a more enlightening afternoon, but when the film became a disappointment she left and attended what was left of the tea party. There she met John (Hally) Huberman, an industrial psychologist, and the attraction was mutual. They were married a year later, on 10 October 1958.

Pentland had never really thought much about marriage. Perhaps it was because her parents had so carefully planned marriage as the culmination of her education. She had managed quite happily on her own to this point, her social life was an active one, and she was giving her full attention to music. It had not occurred to her that it was possible to mix marriage and a career: 'I think most men sensed that I just wasn't interested. It never occurred to me that I would every marry. Early in my life this was the only thing that my parents meant me to do, so I had an innate guard against this happening. The idea that you could get married and still have a career was completely out of my mind, but Hally wanted an independent, self-sufficient wife. I had never met anyone who wanted a professional wife. He is delighted with my success.' Indeed he is. Their wide range of interests includes an active pursuit of one another's careers. Hally came from a musical family and was named after Johannes Brahms; his father, Bronislaw Huberman, had played for Brahms at the age of fourteen. Brahms apparently detested child prodigies but was persuaded to attend this program of his *Violin Concerto* in 1896 and was so impressed he afterwards embraced Bronislaw and sent him a note. Hally's mother, Elza Galafres (she died in 1976 at the age of ninety-seven), was a well-known actress in Berlin and Vienna. Her fascinating autobiography, *Lives, Loves, Losses*, deals with a number of famous lives, including those of two of her husbands – Bronislaw Huberman and the noted pianist, conductor, and composer Ernst von Dohnányi. It was Dohnányi who carefully guided John Huberman's music education. The two were very close, and from 1934–7 they worked together for Hungarian radio. Dohnányi was general music director and Huberman was secretary to the program director, responsible for scheduling performances, including the weekly appearances of Dohnányi as conductor or pianist.

Huberman had a number of careers before finally settling on psychology. He earned a doctorate at the University of British Columbia in 1968 at the age of fifty-seven, first to receive a doctorate in psychology from that institution (and undoubtedly one of the oldest). He is quiet and thoughtful, with a warm and genuine smile and quick wit; their friends are quick to point out that he is just the right complementary match for the aggressiveness in Pentland's personality.

Up to the time of her marriage Pentland had always worked, both from her interest in teaching and because of her need to support herself. Marriage to Huberman removed part of that need. In 1961 her mother died and left an inheritance, which again raised the question of spending so much of her creative energy in the classroom. The final decision to retire from teaching came in 1963. A change in administration at the UBC music department brought about a new approach to the curriculum, one Pentland disagreed with, and that provided the last bit of motivation. She stood firm as usual against what she perceived to be the eroding of academic values, and at the end of the school year she left the university faculty to devote all her time to composing.

7

Second style Part II 1958–1982

Since 1958 Pentland has completed more than fifty compositions. There are works for practically every performance medium: symphony orchestra, chamber ensembles, student works, vocal ensembles, and solo pieces. Since the new style changes of the mid-1950s there has been no dramatic change of direction, but that is not to say Pentland's style has stood still. She has continued to experiment with new approaches and new technical elements, although always within the framework of the serial technique. The flexibility that came with both the new technique and the increased mastery of her craft has resulted in an extremely varied repertory within the general limits of the new style.

At the basis of the new style is the principle of economical use of materials that has continued to guide all her writing, whether it be for solo, quartet, or full orchestra. In *Symphony No. 4* (1959) can be seen the economy of instrumentation as well as the other elements of the new style used in *Symphony for Ten Parts* two years earlier. *Symphony No. 4*, her latest symphony, was commissioned by the Winnipeg Symphony Orchestra with a grant from the Canada Council and was premièred in Winnipeg under the direction of Victor Feldbrill in 1960. For Pentland it was a warm, if somewhat belated recognition by her home town.

Symphony No. 4 is somewhat different from *Symphony for Ten Parts*; it is for full symphonic orchestra rather than chamber ensemble and is written on a much larger scale. In terms of approach to the composition and her treatment of the large orchestra, it stands somewhere between the broad style used in the first two symphonies and the intimate miniature approach of *Symphony for Ten Parts*.

In *Symphony No. 4* there is some use of doubling, but Pentland rarely uses the orchestra as a whole. She uses choirs of instruments and mixtures of sounds in order to realize colour changes and contrasts, but does not resort to the broad dramatic presentation seen in her earlier symphonic works. The opening bars of the first movement are a good example of the kinds of lines and instrument combinations called upon throughout the four movements (see Example 7.1).

The basic material for all movements is stated in the opening bars seen in Example 7.1, although Pentland once again creates four quite different moods with that material. The first movement is agitated and pointillistic as is suggested by the short lines, concise rhythmic phrases, and sudden shifts of instrumentation found in the opening statement. Throughout the movement the short melodic phrases skip furtively from one insrument to another, one range to another, requiring the listener to follow the melodic thread through a myriad of quick colour changes. The first three bars of Example 7.1 are a good example of this: the actual phrase is three bars in length but it skips from the opening high F sharp in violin and flute to a low E in bass strings, bassoon, and timpani at the end of the phrase, passing through three colour changes on the way. The constant shift of colour, rhythm, texture, and pace is along the lines seen in *Symphony for Ten Parts*, but with the greater resources of the full orchestra Pentland is able to make the gestures more dramatic by doubling and octave reinforcement (Example 7.1, bar 7) and by broadening the statements just a bit.

The entire first movement is a constant working-out (development) of the intervals and rhythms found in the opening statement – not the statement as a whole, but the individual two- and three-note groups. The basic energy of this quick-moving movement (*allegro con brio*) is its short and irregular rhythmic patterns, for example the first three cello notes in Example 7.1. A development of this pattern might single out the interval of a fifth for slow or rapid alternation, or merely dwell on the off-the-beat aspect of the first note of the pattern (𝄾 ♪ ♩), for example, stating the rhythm in different instrument colours. The irregular pace and change of texture developed in *Symphony for Ten Parts* is applied here, varying from statements as short as a single note to passages drawn out to three and four measures. The listener is treated to an energetic and constantly changing pattern of rhythms and sound colours, a combination of the delicate pointillism used in *Symphony for Ten Parts* and the massive power of the full orchestral colour in *Symphony No. 2*.

Using the same melodic and harmonic motifs, the second movement is far more lyrical and relaxed, with a principal melody constructed in the

SYMPHONY 4

TO JOHN HUBERMAN

BARBARA PENTLAND

* LIFT FOR REBOUND

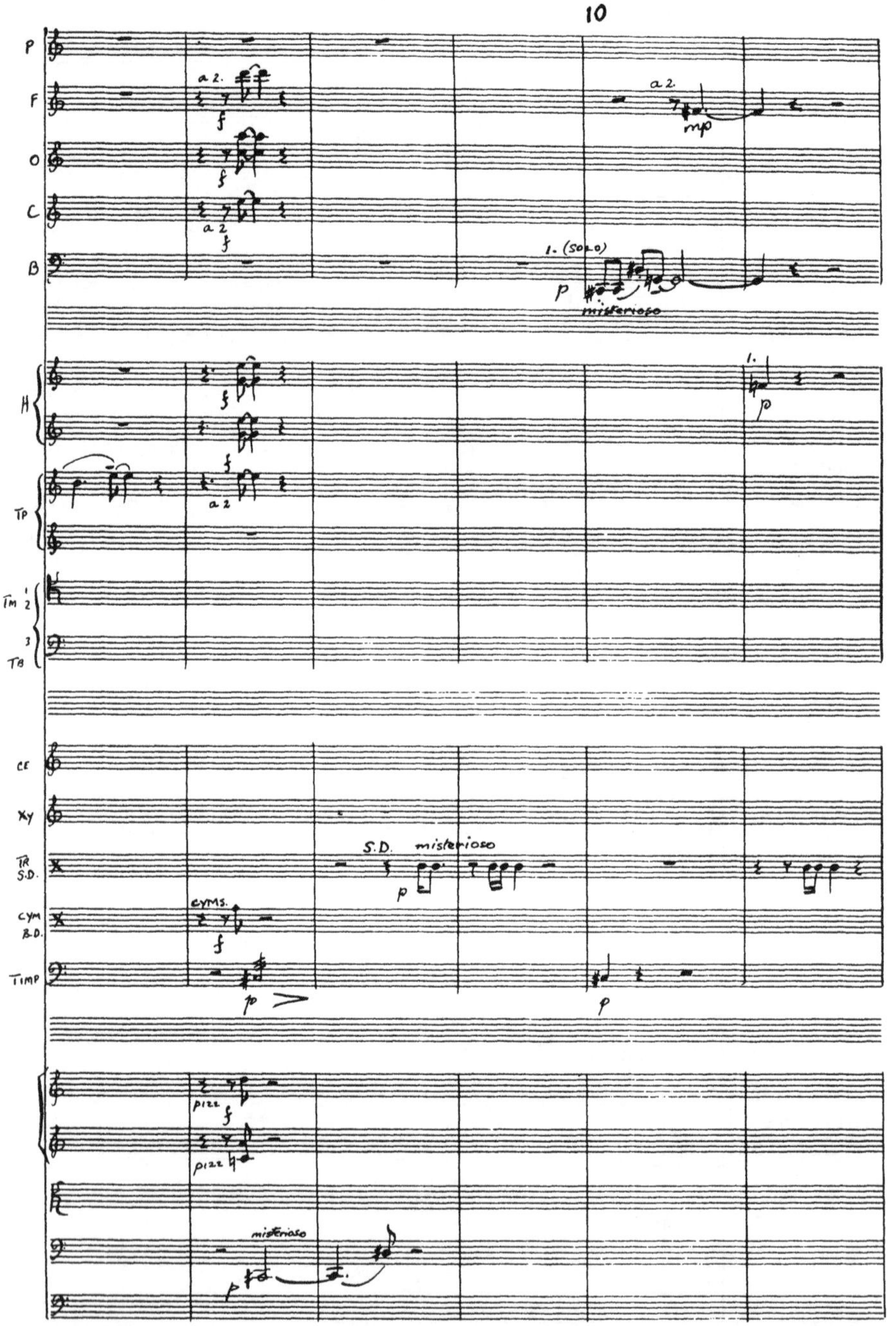

7.1 *Symphony No. 4*, 1st movement, bars 1–11. See p. 84.

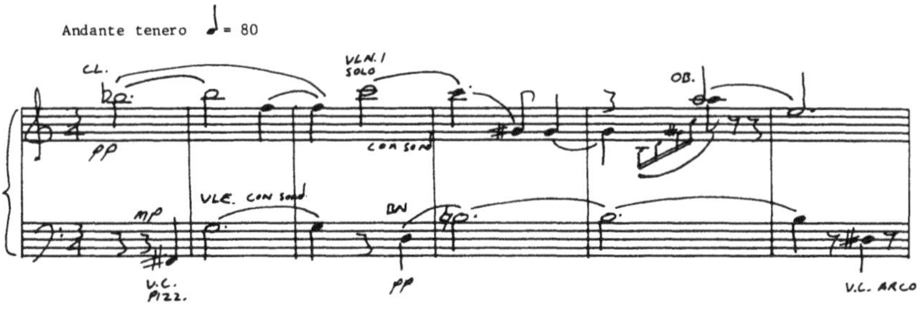

7.2 *Symphony No. 4*, 2nd movement, bars 1–6. See p. 85.

7.3 *Symphony No. 4*, 3rd movement, opening rhythm. See p. 85.

7.4 *Symphony No. 4*, 3rd movement, bars 34–40. See p. 85.

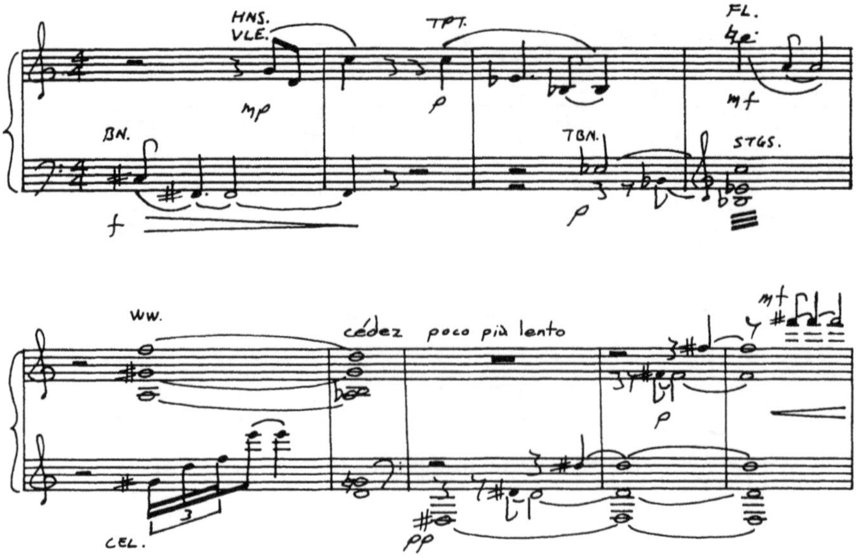

7.5 *Symphony No. 4*, 4th movement, bars 117–25. See p. 85.

fashion of a duet between the woodwinds and the strings (Example 7.2) contrasted with a secondary theme that has the rhythmic pattern  as its major motif. The movement moves from the gentle opening statements to a fairly intense development and combination of the two themes and then returns to the original quiet mood.

For the third movement, called 'vivace umoristico,' Pentland indulges in some broad humour in what she describes as Haydn's attitude towards the scherzo movement. As with so many of her humorous movements, this one is based on quick, catchy rhythmic patterns; the entire movement could be described as development and gradual elaboration of the initial rhythmic pattern entirely presented by percussion (see Example 7.3), which is related to the rhythms found in the opening bars of the first movement (compare Example 7.3 with Example 7.1). This movement contains one of Pentland's most overtly funny passages when, in the midst of the rhythmic development, a trumpet with a wa-wa mute plays a jazz-like passage that mocks the rest of the orchestra (Example 7.4). The actual inspiration for the muted trumpet came from her husband, who has a particular liking for the humourous characteristics of the wa-wa mute. (The symphony is dedicated to him.) As the movement comes to an end in a quasi-mirroring of the opening bars, the percussion section is given a four-bar improvised cadenza, and there is a final loud and ungraceful low B flat sounded by the bassoon.

The last movement is written in an extremely contrapuntal style. The theme is a simple rearrangement of the intervals and rhythms used for the first movement, and therefore its closing passage not only ends the fourth movement but also recalls the opening of the first movement as well. The symphony is brought in a complete circle with a final F sharp (Example 7.5), the note on which it opened.

The fourth movement is a summing up of the material found in the earlier movements. Since the themes for all movements are taken from a common source, Pentland is able to manoeuvre the theme of the movement through development sections in such a way that the themes, rhythms, and even the moods of all the other movements are recalled.

The critical reactions to the première performance in Winnipeg were extreme. Jeffrey Anderson of the *Free Press* (26 Feb 1960) called the work 'tedious and confusing.' He found the humour of the third movement 'particularly vulgar' and decided that the entire work was 'halting.' At the other extreme, S. Roy Maley praised the composition and composer in the *Tribune* (26 Feb), and in a long private letter to Pentland expressed great admiration. The contrasting reactions were at least partly the result of the ways in which they approached the composition. Anderson was familiar with *Studies in Line* and *Symphony No. 2*, and in the review he compared the new work unfavourably to the older two. He was looking for the drive, broad gestures, and continuity of Pentland's first style, and when it was not present he judged *Symphony No. 4* 'halting.' Maley, in contrast, attended the orchestra rehearsals, and in his letter to Pentland confessed that had he not become familiar with the work through repeated hearings, he would not have been able to write a review. He too, on first hearing, was surprised at the new style, but by performance time he had adjusted to 'the astonishing economy of means.'

Chester Duncan, in a review (6 Mar) of the symphony on the CBC program 'Critically Speaking' managed to combine both views. He termed the work 'significant' and reflected on Pentland's objectives: 'With Barbara Pentland it's a matter of honour and necessity to keep composing in the only way one knows how to. And like some heroine in Henry James, her work, in its nuance and scruple, comes up with some form of merit exquisitely incalculable – the cost being to give up being merely attractive and agreeable. The spirit of the *Symphony No. 4* is high and solitary and most stern, and though at this stage one wouldn't attempt to judge it finally, the scoring or rather placing of the materials on the ear is consistently delicate and beautiful. It was music to my ears.' But in spite of his attraction to the work as a whole, he agreed with Anderson about the vulgarity of the third movement. 'Generally speaking one noticed the genteel elevation of the work, but the 3rd movement, I feel, is an embarrassing though significant mistake. Here, it seems to me the composer shows how strained and banal are the results when a high-born maiden longs for the common touch. The movement attempts to walk in the street and only succeeds in falling flat on its face. The grotesque effects of this movement, which were meant to be amusing, nevertheless enhance the general high quality of the other movements.'

A year later (1961), when the symphony was performed in Toronto for the Canadian Conference of the Arts, it met with similar critical reactions. John Beckwith knew what to expect and reported favourably in the *Star* (6 May) that the symphony 'accomplishes what all too few pointillist pieces do, a real sense of themes passing across the orchestra.' George Kidd, in the *Telegram* (6 May), missed the pointillistic intentions of the work (or ignored them) and called it 'a raw work that

7.6 *Canzona for Flute, Oboe and Harpsichord*, p. 1. See p. 87.

7.7 *Canzona for Flute, Oboe and Harpsichord,* bars 87–100. See p. 87.

promises much but is never given the full opportunity to develop into the musical picture it should be ... It deserved the "boo" it received from a solitary but honest gentleman in the audience.' Kidd, like Anderson, was looking for broad statements and missed the more subtle organization picked up by Beckwith, Maley, and Duncan. The combination of old and new techniques in *Symphony No. 4* is unusual but quite successful, and the result is Pentland's most attractive composition for full orchestra; a work equal to her dramatic giants, *News* and *Disasters of the Sun*.

Not all Pentland's compositions from this period use rapid change of instrumental colour as a major element. In *Canzona for Flute, Oboe and Harpsichord* (1961), the three instruments present the thematic material in comparatively long lines. The tone qualities of flute, oboe, and harpsichord are quite contrasting, but in this composition they are combined and woven together rather than separated as are the contrasting sounds in *Symphony for Ten Parts* and *Symphony No. 4*.

The title *Canzona* and the three instruments selected are references to the Baroque period, and indeed the work has a number of associations with the music of the early eighteenth century. Pentland's approach to *Canzona* is similar to the trio-sonata principle of the Baroque era; the two wind instruments are treated as a pair and they expose the thematic material together. (See Example 7.6.) The harpsichord sometimes serves as an accompaniment instrument while the winds treat the theme, and sometimes it joins with the winds or replaces them completely. Pentland's concept of composition from constantly reassembled and varied motifs is quite similar to Baroque compositional practice, and it was therefore an easy step for her to adopt a Baroque attitude for this work. The texture throughout is kept intentionally thin and transparent, and the composer successfully captures the light, dance-like Baroque spirit in a twentieth-century melodic-harmonic idiom.

Canzona, like all her other works after 1950, is founded on the twelve-tone series, but the treatment of the series in a fugal setting of this work is far more rigid than that ordinarily found in a Pentland work. Beginning in bar 87 (Example 7.7), she begins a fugue with the flute. In bar 91 the oboe enters, and in bar 95, the harpsichord. It is immediately obvious that, although the rhythm of the fugue is identical for each of the three entries, the notes are different. What the composer has done is to use a twelve-note series for an eleven-note fugue subject, and as a result the twelfth note of the series is the first note of the next entry. The rhythm remains the same for each entry, but the melody is 'off' by one note. (See Example 7.8.)

This kind of row manipulation bears a close relationship to the devices used by Bach and the others of his era. It is the creative product of both a well-schooled craftsman and a clever inventor. *Canzona* has the same kind of charm and humour as the works Pentland was using as her model. She achieved her goal on several levels and the result is a charming neo-classic trio sonata.

In the summer of 1963 Pentland and her husband spent six weeks travelling through Europe. They visited several countries, enjoying the art and the culture, and then stopped in Budapest.

The visit to Hungary was a return to his birthplace for Pentland's husband. Huberman has been away from his homeland since 1938 and returned now to renew old acquaintances and introduce his new wife. Since his background was so tied to musical circles in Budapest, it was also an opportunity for Pentland to become acquainted with Hungarian musicians. The most interesting of the visits for Pentland was with Zoltan Kodály (1882–1967), who had been a long-time friend of Huberman and had in fact been best man at the wedding of Huberman's mother to Dohnányi. They visited at the apartment of Kodály and his wife, and Pentland was asked to perform one of her works. Knowing Kodály's more conservative writing style she decided it would be safer to play *Studies in Line* than one of her more recent compositions. Kodály had a large Bösendorfer piano that had a small, hinged lid over extra bass keys, and in the midst of Pentland's performance he reached over and raised the lid. She still wonders if this was a joke or a comment on her music. Later, when she remaked about having played a wrong note he replied: 'Are there any wrong notes in contemporary music?'

After a lunch everyone set out in Kodály's government-supplied chauffered car for a trip into the countryside where Huberman had grown up. Everywhere they went Kodály was recognized, and strangers greeted him with a reverential bow. And when they stopped at a coffee-house the gypsy orchestra recognized him and performed with more precision. Pentland could not keep from comparing this treatment of a composer to that given any North American!

The holiday also marked the end of Pentland's formal teaching career at the University of British Columbia. When she returned to Vancouver she could finally devote all her efforts to composing. Shortly after her return she began to experiment with some new colouristic devices in her compositions. Many of the changes in Pentland's compositional tech-

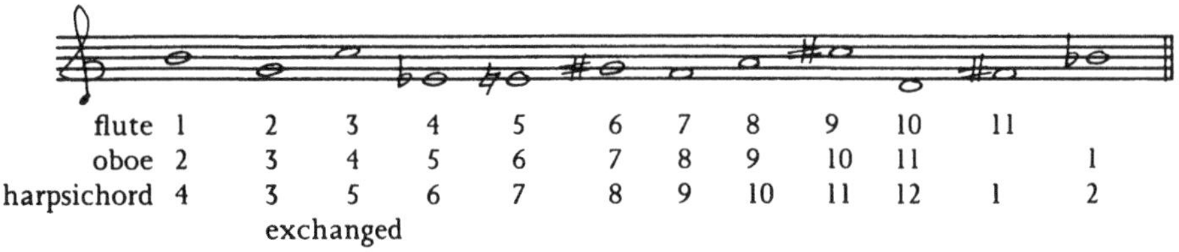

7.8 *Canzona for Flute, Oboe and Harpsichord*, row variant in fugue. See p. 88.

7.9 *Strata*, bars 17–28. See p. 89.

7.10 *Trio con alea*, zone 2. See p. 91.

niques have been linked to trips she took, although the connection in this case probably is quite accidental. Usually there is a direct relationship between events that took place on the trip and the new techniques – a new teacher or perhaps exposure to new works. In this case there is no identifiable cause-and-effect relationship; there is certainly little in the music of Kodály that even remotely resembles Pentland's approach. Colour contrast had been one of the elements that impressed her in the music of Pierre Boulez that she had heard in 1955, and as early as *Symphony for Ten Parts* she had consciously used colour as one of the ingredients in her works. But beginning with *Strata* (1964) she began in earnest to investigate the many ways of using colouristic techniques as a basic part of some of her compositions.

In *Strata* for string orchestra, Pentland uses the instrumental techniques of harmonics, tremolo, glissando, col legno (wood of the bow), sul ponticello (on the bridge), and several other non-traditional sounds which she employed as essential parts of the composition. She divides the strings into two groups, a solo string quartet (two violins, viola, cello), and a larger string orchestra including double bass. The basic concept is similar to the Baroque concerto grosso, and, although there are no sound resemblances, Pentland does begin with the Baroque idea of contrast between the two groups and then expands the possibilities by use of the new sound devices. She envisioned various sound layers – solo vs ensemble, solid tones vs harmonics, vibrato vs non-vibrato tone, as well as layers of melodic and harmonic sounds. The work succeeds as a constantly changing combination of pastels which stop, start, and shimmer, as in Example 7.9. The effect of the new sounds was the addition of a new dimension in developing the musical possibilities of the material. Within the limitations of a string orchestra there were new expressive colour possibilities, as in Example 7.9, bars 17 and 18, where the tremolo sound becomes brittle as it fades, through application of the ponticello technique.

Through the years Pentland has continued to try new ideas and new techniques that she adapts and integrates into her overall style. Perhaps the most interesting new technical addition – and the most radical from Pentland's point of view – was the adoption of the aleatoric principle beginning in the late 1960s.

In 1967 Eugene Wilson was involved in the performance of a work commissioned by the UBC music department. Wilson had been a member of Lukas Foss's improvising ensemble in Los Angeles and asked Pentland to include improvisatory opportunities in the new work. Initially

Pentland resisted. Her method of writing was one of total control, in fact all the technical changes over the previous twenty-five years were for the purpose of achieving maximum control! The proposed improvisatory sections appeared to her to be in total opposition to her way of working. She had always been open to new ideas, however, and after much thought she realized how she could incorporate the new idea into her work without changing style or doing violence to her concept of composition. The result, in 1966, was *Trio con alea* (Trio with chance) for violin, viola, and cello, a four-movement work with nine aleatoric sections that she calls 'zones.'

The following quotation from program notes written by Pentland for a performance of *Trio con alea* gives us her understanding of the technique:

> 'Chance' music has a venerable past. Singers and instrumentalists were expected to decorate or improvise their parts under certain conditions; cadenzas to concertos were improvised and performances included periods of 'free improvisation'.
>
> One may speculate to what extent the upsurge of science at the end of the nineteenth century, with the hope it gave for creating a perfectly predictable world, influenced creative artists towards making performances of their works as predictable as possible through increasingly precise annotations. The advent of radio and the recording devices also called for high levels of exactly determined performance times, technical precision and careful control of sound levels. Chance had to be kept to a minimum.
>
> Heisenberg's 'uncertainty principle', postulated in the 20's, according to which it is impossible to predict accurately the behavior of even ' lifeless' atomic particles, may have started a reversal of this trend. Its waves caught the imagination of artists: if predictability is impossible, why not introduce chance as an organic part of the work?

The last sentence might suggest a fairly free attitude on her part towards an aleatoric composition, but nothing could be further from the truth.

The basic concept of aleatoric music is to give the performers an opportunity to particpate in the creation of the composition through improvisation. There are as many ways to allow this as there are composers, but in general it is up to the composer to decide how much control he will retain and how much freedom he will allow the performer. Such composers as Mauricio Kagel, Karlheinz Stockhausen, Lukas Foss, and, especially, John Cage allow the performer a great amount of freedom in controlling the ultimate shape of a given composition.

That approach is certainly not the one adopted by Pentland. She decided to retain a great deal of control over the composition, and therefore the aleatoric sections offer the performer rather restricted opportunities for improvisation. Example 7.10 illustrates the freedom and the restrictions of a typical aleatoric section in *Trio con alea*.

In this section all performers are allowed rhythmic freedom, but for the viola, rhythm is the only freedom; the dynamics, pitches, and general speed are all stated by the composer. For the two other instruments there is a bit more freedom. The mark ⟶ ∿∿∿ indicates that the notes are to be played in order first, but may be combined in any sequence on repeat; –⊓–∨– allows the performers a choice of bowing; and –++++– gives the performer a choice of single or multiple stops. The dynamic levels and general rate of speed, however, are stated. The decisions left to the performers in this example therefore, are tone colour, actual speed, some dramatic realizations, and sequence of notes after the initial statement of the material. The composer has controlled the overall dynamics and all the notes (but not their order after first statement or the combinations of sounds among the parts). For the performers this is an opportunity to use some creative imagination within the restrictions, and for the composer it is control of most of the elements of sound. Pentland has kept a very tight rein over the composition by two factors: by the amount of specific direction given to the performers, and, equally important, by careful selection of the places where she will allow the performers these freedoms. In general, she selects for aleatoric zones those places where the essential elements of the composition have already been firmly established, and where a dramatic or colour section is needed that does not depend for its effect upon those specifics she releases to the performers.

Pentland's second style allows for a freedom with twelve-tone series sequence anyway, and because she establishes the initial sequence of interval cells, little can happen in the aleatoric zone to alter the progress of the composition. By the time any extensive zone appears, the performers have been steeped in the rhythmic and stylistic elements peculiar to that composition. Good taste and the line of least resistance would dictate that they select for their improvisatory passages those rhythmic elements that are compatible with what has been written for them earlier by the composer, thus all but assuring her of stylistic consistency.

The first movement of *Trio con alea* is composed with the basic cells of a seventh (first two notes in the cello), and a minor third (harmonically between cello and viola in bar 2, melodically in violin, bar 4), and a ninth. Two other elements figure heavily: successive entries, although the order is not important (cello, viola, violin in the opening bars; viola, cello, violin in bar 7), and the long fall at the end of each phrase – usually a ninth. (See Example 7.11.)

By the time the opportunity to improvise arrives in zone 2 (Example 7.10), after sixty bars of Pentland's tight compositional style (zone 1 is quite short and very restricted), there is little risk of loss of control by the composer. The notes, which the performers must play in prescribed order first, emphasize the melodic cells of the initial row. The tone row is presented at the beginning of the composition by the cello – the dominant instrument in the piece – with the exception of note 3, which is in the viola part (compare Example 7.12 with Example 7.11), and it is this material, the row, that is the material given to the performers for their improvisatory sections. The cello line in zone 2 is a retrograde version of the initial row, beginning a perfect fifth lower (compare Example 7.12 with Example 7.13). The violin series is an inversion beginning on E, and the viola a retrograde on D. The instruments are furnished, therefore, not only with the melodic cells, those intervals that are important to the structure of the piece, but also the cells are presented melodically in their initial relationship to one another as controlled by the row. Although there is some variation open to the performers, they are tied tightly to the composed material.

In her first aleatoric venture Pentland felt the need also to provide a written description of the aleatoric sections. Before each movement the individual zones are described in detail. Here description of zone 2 is as follows (compare with Example 7.10):

All instruments improvise on given pitches, first in order, then freely repeating ad lib. The violin leads in changing improvising material; the viola and the cello follow in that order, indicated by dotted bars. This is not rigid, and the violin can wait at the pause over the rest symbol until the viola reaches its 'marcato' motif, and sim. The different tempi of the instruments are controlled by several factors: length of rests, amount of repetition, type of rhythmic motifs used and attention to other parts in the order given, adjusting when necessary. At bar 62 the cello reaches tempo giusto, re-entering the regular section; the others may overlap, finishing their improvising in this bar before resting.

7.11 *Trio con alea*, bars 1–10. See p. 92.

7.12 *Trio con alea*, tone row. See p. 92.

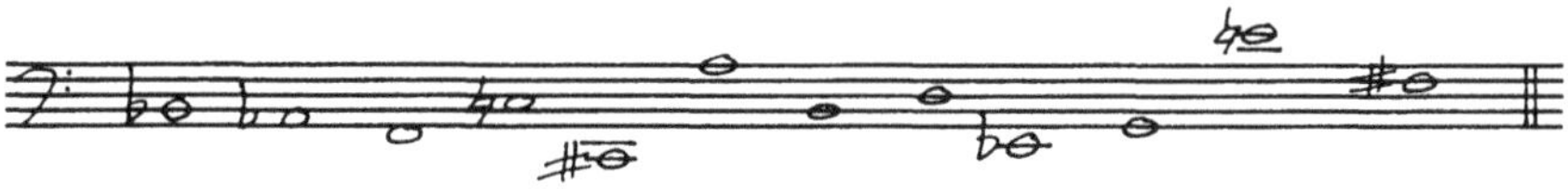

7.13 *Trio con alea*, retrograde row. See p. 92.

ZONE 2:
Brooding mood; tempo and dynamics increase gradually.
LENTO → poco a poco accel. . .
colla voce
(enter after piano)
repeat until string entries. (at random)
repeat until string entries. (at random)
I con sord.
[Cue: piano 2nd tone (C#)]
S.D. c.c.
Perc.
LENTO → poco a poco accel. .
colla voce
[a small descending slide in fade-out.]
ad lib.
(R)RAW
GUER-R-R-RE
(voice tacet)
Ped.
Vlns
Vlas
C.
D.b.
ZONE 2:
entries in numbered order; vertical arrows indicate cues.

7.14 *News*, pp. 6 and 7. See p. 93.

ZONE 2
Sim. to previous passage: continually increasing tempo and dynamic:–
[Parts randomize except for entries]
sim.
secco
poco a poco accel. e cresc. – –
poco a poco accel. e cresc. – – –
sempre accel. e cresc. –
(mf)
(mf)
poco ped. ad lib.
sempre accel. e cresc.

7.15 *Mutations*, zone 2. See p. 94.

7.16 *String Quartet No. 3*, 3rd movement, bars 1–20. See p. 94.

This description is clear evidence of her fear of losing control. In later compositions she eliminated this kind of description after realizing that the musicians could understand the notation.

In the works written since *Trio con alea*, aleatoric sections have become a fairly frequent technique; and she has used them successfully in works for both small and large ensembles. The treatment of the free sections in all those works is similar to that found in *Trio con alea*: the aleatoric material is confined to use of the melodic-harmonic cells of the series, and the zones are found always at a position where preparation has been carefully made for rhythmic improvisation on the given material. Because of Pentland's freedom towards the use of series material, at these points a liberal association fits easily into the flow of the work, given the controls the composer maintains. The transition from composed to aleatoric section is fairly smooth, and if the performers are sensitive to style, the audience should not be aware of what has occurred; the movement as a whole should give the impression of the usual kind of Pentland technique, with tightly integrated elements. The performers, of course, must understand the basic idea of aleatoric writing. Pentland was shocked at a rehearsal of *Cinéscene* (1968) to hear one musician disregard the notes given to him in an aleatoric zone and begin to improvise Czech folk tunes! The performer obviously had not been trained in modern improvisatory techniques, a part of performer training more and more frequently found in enlightened music schools in recent years.

The improvisatory device is for the most part a soloist's technique, and when writing aleatoric sections in works with large ensembles, such as *Disasters of the Sun* (1976), *Cinéscene* (1968), and *News* (1970), Pentland usually restricts the extended aleatoric sections to a few soloists, as in Example 7.28 below, although for dramatic effect she has used the entire orchestra in one of these sections, as in Example 7.14. This ensemble improvisation section in *News* occurs just after the opening statement of the piece. The message in the text is that the news of the day centres around war and other atrocities, and in the quoted example Pentland intends for the orchestra to set the attitude of the scene, which is one of brutality and horror. The notes given to the instruments follow various permutations of the original series, but once the strings begin their glissandi the listener will be aware only of a noise-filled crescendo. The assignment of specific notes at that point has little to do with any consciousness of series; it serves only to guard against the possibility of the musicians selecting tonal passages (or Czech folk tunes). The trumpet fanfare figure is heard earlier, where the part is presented as a solo.

Of all Pentland's works, the one containing the most aleatoric freedom is *Mutations* for cello and piano, commissioned by the CBC in 1972 for Eugene Wilson and Robert Rogers. It was at Wilson's request that Pentland first wrote aleatoric sections in *Trio con alea*, and Rogers, one of Pentland's former UBC students, had performed her works for many years. The quantity of freedom in *Mutations* is a demonstration of her confidence in Wilson and Rogers, who could be counted on to reproduce the Pentland style within the bounds of larger free sections. Even in this work, however, the composer does not leave any of the composition's essence to the performers. The row and the melodic-harmonic-rhythmic cells are carefully laid out for twenty-one bars before the first aleatoric zone begins, and the free section is a natural consequence of those bars. The difference in *Mutations* is really only the size of the zones and the amount of restricted freedom given within them. (See Example 7.15.)

During the composition of *Mutations* Pentland received some unexpected help from a large group of starlings. She was attempting to create a dramatic effect and was having a difficult time with the musical representation. Suddenly, hundreds of starlings alighted in the trees in front of her studio and made a very loud noise. After a few minutes their leader flew off, leavng behind him absolute and sudden silence which just as suddenly reverted to noise when he returned a few seconds later. It was exactly what Pentland was looking for, and, although the sounds she created in zone 2 (Example 7.15) have nothing to do with starling sounds, the passage before bar 86 produces a dramatic effect much like the one created by the birds.

Pentland's experimentation with new sounds continued throughout the 1960s. While working on *Strata* in 1964 she had noted how particularly adaptable were string instruments to the new devices, and in her *String Quartet No. 3* (1969) she included more, this time working with variations of the standard Western divisions of pitch. In this string quartet she includes: quarter-tone sharp (𝄲), three-quarter-tone sharp (𝄰), quarter-tone flat (𝄳), three-quarter-tone flat (𝄭), and variable-width vibrato (〰) (see Example 7.16). As with the earlier devices introduced in *Strata*, these are used as additional ways of exploring the sound potential of the melodic and harmonic elements of the composition. In *String Quartet No. 3* a large part of the musical objective

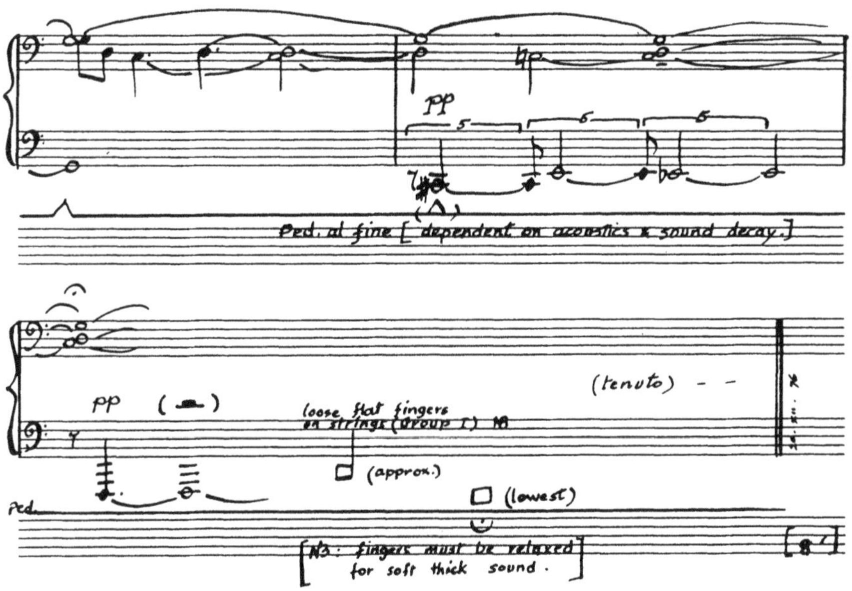

7.17 *Tenebrae*, last three bars. See p. 95.

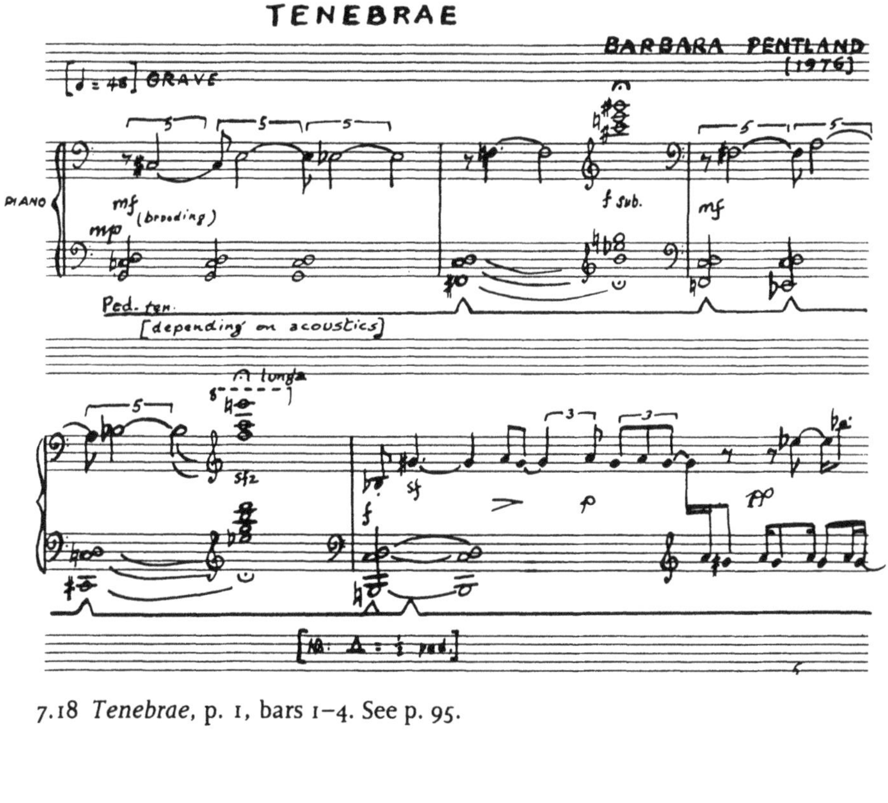

7.18 *Tenebrae*, p. 1, bars 1–4. See p. 95.

7.19 *String Quartet No. 3*, 1st movement, p. 1, bars 1–9. See p. 95.

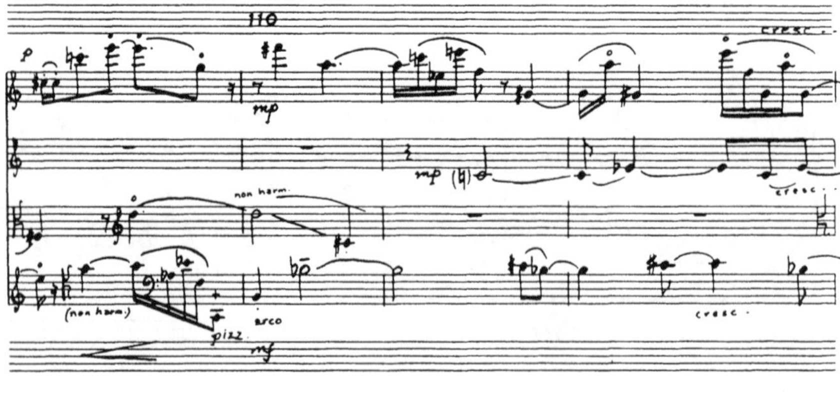

7.20 *String Quartet No. 3*, 1st movement, bars 109–117. See p. 96.

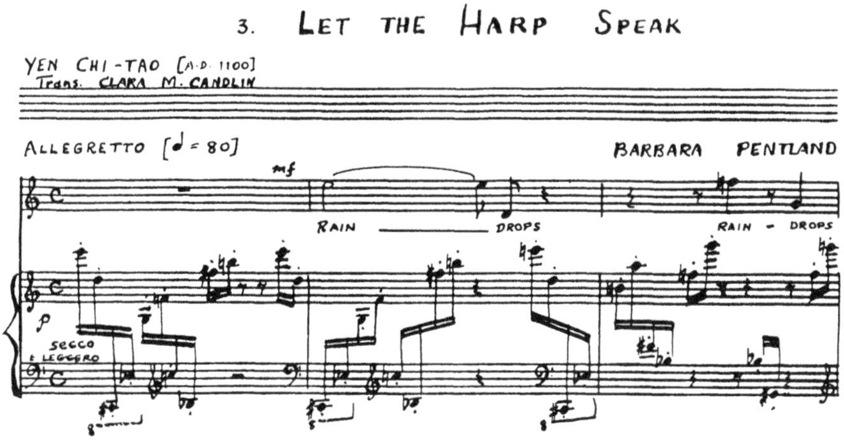

7.21 *Sung Songs, Let the Harp Speak*, bars 1–3. See p. 97.

7.22 *Sung Songs, Midnight among the Hills*. See p. 97.

7.23 *Sung Songs*, *Wanderer's Woe*, bars 1–10. See p. 97.

7.23 *Sung Songs, Wanderer's Woe,* bars 41–49. See p. 97.

consists of development of the motifs through tone variation, and the new devices are therefore an essential part of the composition. In some works these new sound variations are to be considered ornaments on the essential material of the music. The importance of the various devices changes, of course, depending on the particular orientation of each work, but often Pentland considers them non-structural, as for example in *Disasters of the Sun*, Example 7.29 below. At the same time, several works are dominated by a concern for colour, for example, *Strata*, *Angelus* (Ephemera 1) (1977), *String Quartet No. 3*, *Tenebrae* (1976), *Ēventa* (1978), and *String Quartet No. 4* (1980), and in other works colour is important, but to a lesser degree, as in *News*, *Suite Borealis* (1966), *Mutations*, and *Disasters of the Sun*.

Another of her sound explorations has taken her to the inside of the piano – a technique developed in the first half of this century by Henry Cowell (with rather spectacular results in *The Banshee*). Again, this is just another aspect of tone colour in a work in which moods are represented by sound colours. Example 7.17 shows the last bars of *Tenebrae*, and the sounds made by striking the strings with 'loose flat fingers' help to depict the otherworldliness suggested by the title.

Pentland thinks of *Tenebrae* (darkness, shades of death) as a struggle between the first musical element, which she refers to as a 'black cloud' (bars 1–3 in Example 7.18), and its opposing element, loud excitement that continues to try to escape, found at the end of bars 2 and 3. As the work unfolds, the excited element takes up longer and longer periods but is finally overcome by the 'black cloud' (see Example 7.17).

The contrasting colours are heightened by the use of sustained pedal in the slower sections that literally 'clouds' the sonority, and by the use of the inside of the piano in a way that adds another indefinite (=filmy, cloudy) colour. Against this, the rapid motion, accentuated punctuations, and silence of the rebellious element stand in sharp contrast. The work is one of Pentland's most programmatic instrumental works, portraying the last protests of a living spirit before succumbing.

The colour in *String Quartet No. 3* is more complex and less programmatic. By emphasizing colour more sharply Pentland is able to get variety from the tiniest of elements. The central motifs of the first movement are the interval of a seventh, both melodically and harmonically, the rhythm ♫♩, and the sequential entries of the different instruments. One method used for variation of the elements can be seen in two forms in the opening few bars of the movement in Example 7.19.

The interval of a seventh is inverted to a second in bar 3, viola, and then developed by narrowing it to a quarter-tone. This is further varied in bar 6, cello, where an increasingly wider vibrato is indicated, which can be interpreted as a development or variation of the quarter-tone idea. The entire movement revolves around the development of the tiny initial melodic, harmonic, and rhythmic motifs to which colour change adds another full dimension. Example 7.20 shows an unusually dense use of colour effects, in which all the musical elements – seventh, ♫♩ rhythm, and sequential entry – are elaborated, extended, and developed by means of the new colouristic devices.

The other three movements of this quartet are similarly frugal in terms of melodic, rhythmic, and harmonic motifs, and just as rich in the exploration of colouristic effects. The motifs used in each movement are closely related to one another (compare Example 7.16 and Example 7.19), and Pentland further unifies the composition by beginning each movement with material found at the end of the previous movement. At the end of the last movement the motifs from the first movement evolve, creating a truly circular structure in which each movement suggests the next.

Pentland's songs of the 1960s and 1970s should also be mentioned in a discussion of her interest in colour and mood. She has not written a large amount of music for voice. Some of her larger works, *News* and *Disasters of the Sun*, include solo voice, but vocal solo and ensemble have not been an area of much concentration. In her most recent period there have been only two sets of songs, one for solo voice and piano and one for quartet (or chorus), both entitled *Sung Songs*. It is not that Pentland prefers instrumental writing, but she has experienced some difficulty reconciling her second style with the voice. She believes that the biggest problem has been finding texts with which she can work – short, simple, direct lyrics that do not have their own musical rhythm – and that kind of poetry is not easily found.

In 1968 she was invited to contribute music for the new hymnbook to be published jointly by the Anglican and United churches of Canada. The committee sent her twenty-eight texts from which to choose, but she returned them all with a letter of regrets. She found them 'much too verbose to fit any but a late XIX century melody.' She outlined her difficulties in searching for suitable texts and explained that for this reason 'so many composers today, including myself, have turned for song texts to simple translations of ancient Chinese and Japanese lyrics.'

For the *Sung Songs* texts she chose a set of Chinese poems translated by Clara M. Candlin, which contain all the elements mentioned above, and in setting them she approached each song as an opportunity to paint a single mood.

The solo songs were written at different times, the first three in 1964 and two more in 1971, and although they are approached in a similar manner, different technical devices are used to achieve the moods in the two different sets. In the first three songs the vocal parts are rather rhythmically disjunct – short phrases with individual notes separated by short rests. The piano part is in constant motion and is the source of the continual mood colour, while the voice represents the individual word or phrase as the text proceeds, as for example in song 3, *Let the Harp Speak*, where the accompaniment cleverly suggests both a harp and the opening word 'raindrops.' (See Example 7.21.)

In songs 4 and 5, Pentland changes her emphasis and relies on the voice as much as the piano for the continuous motion of the song. The melodic phrases are longer, the texture more varied and she exploits the other colour devices she had developed in the intervening years: quarter-tones, extremes of dynamics, and some keyboard sounds such as pedal blur and tremolo. (See Example 7.22.) Rather than separating the voice and piano parts from one another as in *Let the Harp Speak*, the later songs integrate the two parts. In *Midnight among the Hills*, the voice and piano share many of the same melodic and rhythmic motifs. Instead of vocal line with accompaniment, there is a unified expression using two different instruments, more along the lines of her instrumental works in which the material glides deftly back and forth from one performer to another.

When writing her other set of *Three Sung Songs* for vocal ensemble (1964–5) Pentland looked to the Renaissance for her stylistic model, much as she had done in her earlier choral works. The songs, of course, do not have the sound of the Renaissance, but the formal aspects and treatment of the voices show that she had consciously gone back to her love of early music as she had in *Leisure*, *A Picture*, and *Cradle Song*, written in 1938, after first becoming acquainted with the early repertory while at Juillard. Many of the points of description for these works would also closely describe a number of four-part vocal compositions from the sixteenth century. In *Wanderer's Woe*, for example, she uses a stock sixteenth-century madrigal device to represent the opening word, 'alone' (see Example 7.23). A single voice (the tenor at that!) sings 'alone,' which is the time-honoured method of 'painting' that word. The song proceeds throughout its length as a series of imitated phrases, much the same as a madrigal, with the various voices entering one at a time, each having material similar to that of the first voice to enter. Even the device of mirror writing at the end of the song is in the sixteenth-century style; the last ten bars are an approximate mirror of the first ten (see Example 7.23).

Although Pentland has not written an opera since *The Lake* in 1952, she has composed two quasi-dramatic works; *News* (1970) and *Disasters of the Sun* (1976) were conceived for concert rather than staged performance. Both works contain all the elements of the second style, including the colouristic devices, but there is also a new element: the composer's social commentary, exhibited not only in the choice of text, but in the musical settings.

War horrifies Pentland. Her earliest works with social commentary were reactions to the world wars: *Ruins (Ypres, 1917)* (1932), *Lament* (1934), *Rhapsody 1939*, subtitled *The World on the March to War Again*, and a second *Lament* (1939). *News*, for virtuoso voice and orchestra, is Pentland's heart-felt emotional reaction to violence of all kinds, especially that of the Viet Nam war and the racial conflicts in the United States at the end of the 1960s. She began *News* in 1968 when the atrocities of war were regularly reported in the news media with an attitude of acceptance. It was also a time of constant reports of violence in the cities and the first real awareness of air pollution. To Pentland it seemed that North America was intent on self-destruction, and what was worse, the newspapers, news magazines, and radio and television newscasts all reported the events as indifferently as they would a garden party.

The text for *News* is entirely from normal news sources, including CBC news, BBC news, the Associated Press, the Montreal *Gazette*, the *New York Times*, and the Manchester *Guardian*. The phrases are pieced together for their contrast and dramatic effect. 'The only way I could react musically was by facing these now frequent reports with satire, scorn and in some cases, flippancy.' After completing the first third of the composition, the horror of the world situation discouraged her, and she put it aside. But in 1970 the CBC offered to commission a serious social commentary, and she finished the work, still depressed by the state of the world, which had not changed in the intervening two years.

In composing *News*, Pentland called upon all the technical and colouristic devices she had worked with earlier in the decade, including quarter-tones, *Sprechstimme* (half-spoken), aleatoric zones, and even a few new sounds her soloist, Phyllis Mailing, interpolated. There is a large amount of variety in the musical setting: for those kinds of reports

7.24 *News*, p. 1. See p. 99.

p
mf
-- N--- N N--- N N N N N New----------------s swen-----
(n) All the news that's fit------ to print?
Tif staht swen-- eht (u)ll--- a Ha ha ha ha
f
ad lib.
(small descending slide in fade out)
War---------------------- (R) Raw----------- Guer-r-r-re
(roll)

7.25 *News*, bars 7–18, voice; bars 23–29. See p. 99.

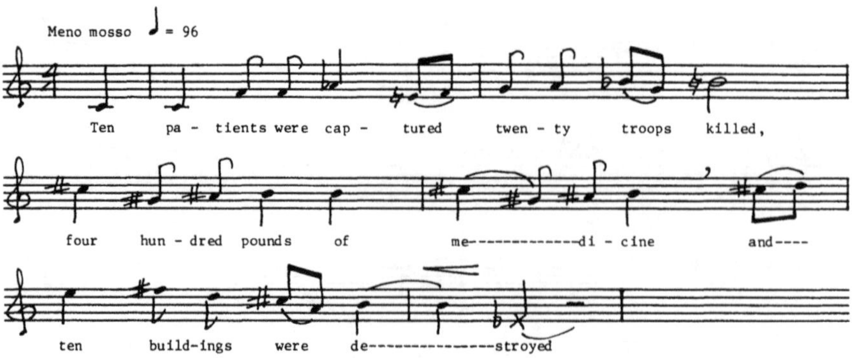

7.26 *News*, bars 408–414, voice. See p. 99.

that were repetitive she chose a quasi-plain-chant treatment; for another, a child's nursery rhyme to symbolize the 'unbelievable' qualities of the information; and in several places she quotes from well-known music to express sarcasm. The result is her most dramatic and intense composition to date.

The primary musical motif for *News* is appropriately a representation of the sound of the teletype machine, a staccato irregular rhythm on a single pitch (Example 7.24). The selection of this sound for the principal motif is ingenious: it is symbolic of the news media and so flexible it can be used in practically any melodic, harmonic, or rhythmic setting; and the very nature of a repeated pitch adds to the dramatic intensity of the overall message. Pentland uses the motif in a variety of ways: as initially stated in the percussion, bar 1, suggestive of the teletype; as a portion of a trumpet fanfare, bar 4; as a way of mocking the word 'news' in the vocal line; and as an accompaniment figure to a number of different vocal phrases (for the last two uses of the motif see Example 7.25).

Pentland communicates her opinion as aggressively and broadly as possible, beginning with the distortion of the first word of the text, 'news,' followed immediately by the motto of the *New York Times*, 'All the news that's fit to print,' which she derides by stating it backwards, followed by bitter laughter (Example 7.25). The mirror technique is employed a number of times for text and music as a display of scorn. In some cases word mirroring even yields interesting word associations: war=raw; bomb=(b)mob; and she also plays on words by separating the syllables, as in 'sh-he-hell' for the word 'shell' (see Example 7.25). The work fairly drips with sarcasm: 'Tens of thousands of terrified civilians / number of homeless staggering proportions / Et in terra pax hominibus bonae voluntatis [and on earth peace to men of good will].' The musical setting for the above passage is chant-like for emphasis. At another point the *Dies irae* (Day of wrath), a chant from the mass for the dead, is used as background; and for a setting of an enumeration of war destruction she chooses the melody of *The Twelve Days of Christmas* (Example 7.26). Other musical quotations also used for satire are from *Let My People Go* and *America the Beautiful*. The colouristic devices are put to good programmatic use accentuating the drama of the text, as in the use of aleatoric sections to allude to chaos (see Example 7.14). At other places aleatoric zones allow the performers to help shape a dramatic moment, and quarter-tones and *Sprechstimme* intensify the satire and heighten the drama.

There is nothing subtle about Pentland's message in *News*; no subtlety was intended. She found the world's condition brutal and her commentary was in keeping with Chester Duncan's 1940 defence of her *Lament*: as an artist she observed the society and reacted to it honestly. The intensity and vehemence of her composition are a direct reflection of her reaction.

The other dramatic work, *Disasters of the Sun* (1976), for mezzo soprano and nine players, has a different kind of message. *Disasters* is no less an artistic success than *News*, but the attitude and general approach taken by Pentland are quite different. In place of the bold and intense statements in *News*, *Disasters* is more emotionally varied and less broad in its presentation – a difference reflected even in the comparatively smaller performing forces required.

The text is based on a cycle of seven poems by Dorothy Livesay (librettist for *The Lake*), the first English-language poetry Pentland had found both modern and flexible enough to work with. Livesay was teaching at the University of Victoria and had been present at the first performance of *Mutations* in Vancouver in 1973. She was impressed by Pentland's newest style developments and sent her the *Disasters* poems. Pentland recognized them as the kind of text she had been looking for and set to work on them immediately. The text expresses a sentiment near to the hearts of both Livesay and Pentland: women's struggle in a man's world. *Disasters* is the only work to date in which Pentland has expressed her feelings concerning sexual oppression, although she has been partial to women in several other ways throughout her career: the leading character in *The Lake* is a woman, and the texts for many, but not all, of her vocal works are by women. In *Disasters*, feminism is portrayed symbolically by the opposition of the Sun and the Moon. The Sun represents male domination; it determines life and death. The Moon (woman) is its opposite, the need for water and security. Pentland describes her own feelings: 'It's still very much a male dominated world, women fit into a pattern (and of course I don't). They are expected to suppress themselves. The world is still terribly dominated by men. Only occasionally does a woman get listened to. It comes home to me with a shock sometimes.'

She set the seven poems in seven songs or movements, each one quite different in mood, representing the sentiment of the text. The first song is angry and challenges the dominance of the Sun; songs 2 and 4 are more calm statements, less antagonistic and more philosophical; 3 is flippant; 5 builds into an exaggerated drama for the words 'constant danger'; 6 is march-like, suggesting the 'tyrannical king'; and the last song is an epilogue similar to a lament. Pentland retains the poetry intact, but in songs 4 and 7, she augments the text by echo on pre-recorded tape (shown at right).

1

O you old
gold garnered
incredible sun
sink through my skin
into the barren bone

If I'm real
I'm totem carved
with your splayed
scalpel

If I'm a person
the gods roar
in horrible surprised
masculinity

but if I'm a woman
paint me
with the beast stripes
assure me I am human

2

The world is round
it is an arm
a round us
my fingers touching Africa
your hand
tilting Siberian trees
our thoughts
still as the tundra stones
awaiting footprints

bright between our bones
shines the invisible sun

3

Though I was certain
we recognized each other
I could not speak:
the flashing fire
between us
fanned no words

In the airport circle   where
the baggage tumbled
all my jumbled life
fumbled
to find the one sweet piece
in the clothing stuffed and duffled
labelled mine

and over across the circle saw
your dark hair, piercing eyes
lean profile, pipe in mouth.

Incredibly, you move.
You seem to dance
and suddenly
you stand beside me, calm
without surprise:

I cannot tell
what country you are from
we recognize each other
and are dumb

your hand   your hand
tense on your pipe
your look   a soft bomb
behind my eyes

4

My hands that used to be leaves
tender and sweet and soothing
have become roots
gnarled in soil

my hands
tender as green leaves
blowing on your skin
pulling you up
into joyous air
are knotted bones
whitening in the sun

My hands leaves

Gnarled in soil

My hands
tender as green leaves

5

During the last heat wave
a sunflower
that had stood up straight
outstaring the June
sun
wilted   collapsed
under a pitiless July
sky

now in burning August
I close out the city
trembling under heat
the green trees visibly
paling –

I close and curtain off myself
into four walls
breezed by a fan
but the fan
fumes!
and suddenly it
BREAKS OFF   from the wall
whirls   across the room
to rip my forefinger.

I tell you
we live in constant
danger
under the sun   bleeding
I tell you

6

Keep out
keep out of the way of
this most killing
northern sun
grower   destroyer

Sun, you are no goodfather
but tyrannical king:
I have lived sixty years
under your fiery blades
all I want now
is to grope for those blunt
moon scissors

7

When the black sun's
gone down
connect me underground:
root tentacles
subterranean water

Black sun

no more lovely man can be
than he with moon-wand
who witches water

If I'm a woman
Assure me
I am human

In setting the poems Pentland once again called on musical quotation, although not to the extent that she did in *News*. In the opening movement she mocks the sun by distorting a quotation of what is to her the musical epitome of male dominance, the theme from Strauss's *Don Juan* (see Example 7.27). In song 3, the duet 'La ci darem la mano' from Mozart's *Don Giovanni* is quoted to evoke the images of a dance, and of seduction, and song 7 is built on both the ground bass and some melodic

35
ZONE 1
TEMPO GIUSTO
TACET
TACET
TACET
BELLS
omit high if not on instrument.
Cue: singer "roar" (follow) after
MARIMBA:
mf
f
mp
PERC
TACET
p
PNO.
sempre pp
Cue: after "roar"
Stand holding R. Ped.
stroke lowest string group inside piano
(keys)
[sit]
(tenuto)
(approx.)
low
To HORN
Ped. Ped.
Ped. - off
ZONE 1
TEMPO GIUSTO
follow piano string gliss.
at least 5"
gods
r-r-r-roar r-r-r-r
in hor-r-r-rible
sur- prised
VN
VA
C

7.27 *Disasters of the Sun*, bars 35–41. See p. 104.

DISASTERS OF THE SUN

DOROTHY LIVESAY

BARBARA PENTLAND

7.28 *Disasters of the Sun*, bars 1–4, 10–14. See p. 105.

fragments from Dido's lament from Purcell's opera *Dido and Aeneas*. These quotations, however, are just incidental devices used to suggest moods and attitudes, and in the case of the *Don Juan* and *Don Giovanni* quotes, to lighten the composition for a moment in a typically Pentland fashion. (She does the same kind of thing to lighten an overly serious conversation.) In context, these quotations lend themselves easily to the drama of the work and blend in well with the overall composition.

The technical organization of this work is so complex that it allows for endless analysis. A work of this length, approximately thirty minutes, contains a fairly large number of motifs; there are seven major motifs, all of which appear in the opening statement (see Example 7.28). The motifs are marked in the example (the numbers do not suggest relative importance):

1 decoration of a single note (E flat in this example)
2 shimmering sound (tremolo in bar 2)
3 falling line over a wide range
4 interval of a ninth
5 interval of a third (major and minor)
6 three equal notes on the same pitch
7 piano clusters

The seventh motif, piano clusters, is employed as a symbol of the sun and is used to evoke the image of the sun when it appears in the text or when it is implied, similar to the use of the leitmotif for the monster in *The Lake*. The use of major and minor thirds symbolizes to the composer the physical shape of the world; the roundness of the world is represented constantly by the thirds which turn around one another throughout the composition. In a composition so full of symbolism the existence of seven major motifs may be related to the seven movements of the composition, although Pentland denies any intentional connection.

In this work, as in *News*, the colouristic devices of *Sprechstimme*, quarter-tones, and aleatoric zones are used to achieve those dramatic effects which are not in need of specific notation, or which in some cases cannot possibly be notated exactly (as in Example 7.29). The word 'gnarled' in bar 224 is delivered onomatopoeically in *Sprechgesang*, emphasizing the 'r,' and in aleatoric zone 5 the word 'up' is represented by an ascending line without a clear pitch for the last note. Similarly, 'blowing' is sung to a wavy melodic line with a glissando at the end, and the quarter-tones for 'skin' give the word a sensuous character. Throughout the composition the instruments support the picturesque words by echoing the sound effects of the voice and reinforcing the images. The tape-recorded part, seen in Example 7.29, is Pentland's way of allowing the singer to 'reflect,' a method of representing yet another dimension in the composition; the soloist pre-records specific portions of the work and they are played back during performance at points marked in the score.

The Livesay poems make a good match for Pentland's music. The text offers clean, short statements that are direct and hard-hitting yet full of colourful imagery – a description that also fits Pentland's musical style of the 1970s. The musical setting supports the text by giving it additional dimensions; lending firm instrumental support to the direct statements such as 'Sun, you are no goodfather but tyrannical king' in song 6, and providing a more detached and colourful image for the description of the sunflower wilting in the sun, in song 5.

Pentland saw in the text a clear image of her own life. The quotation from *Don Juan* (see Example 7.27), to set the word 'masculinity,' is superficially humorous, but to Pentland it is far more meaningful. Beneath the joke there is her impression that much of the struggle she has had as a composer has been directly related to men trumpeting their 'masculinity.' The 'tyrannical king' rejected in the poem represents those who have attempted to suppress her and her work.

The last poem, the Moon's reaction to final triumph, is set to the model of Dido's lament from Purcell's opera of 1689. Both the music and Dido's words, 'When I am laid in earth, may my wrongs create no trouble,' seemed to Pentland a mood similar to Livesay's final statement. After a lifetime of struggling against Sun's tyranny, the Moon could relax with a quiet, introspective moment.

Disasters of the Sun is rightly considered one of Pentland's finest works; it attests to her unceasing growth as a composer. The work was commissioned by the Vancouver New Music Society and had its première at a concert in honour of Pentland's sixty-fifth birthday in 1977. It is typical of Pentland's committment to her art that a celebration for her would have to be a celebration of her music; and it is also typical of her personality that a birthday celebration for her would involve a gift *from* her to the musical world. Nothing could represent Pentland any better than that event. The text, the music, and the constant giving through music all speak for her.

Pentland's most recent compositions suggest that she is currently headed in yet another direction. In *Ēventa* (1978) and *String Quartet*

No. 4 (1980), she uses the colouristic devices to a greater extent than in the past, bringing to these works a new level of abstraction. A description of the musical elements of these pieces is similar to that for earlier compositions – dissonant intervals guided by a tone row, and short rhythmic motifs – but the use and development of these elements are more abstract. Throughout the entire 'second style' period Pentland has tended towards more economy and concise statement, and with that in mind it can be seen that these two latest works follow logically. Example 7.30 illustrates the amount of complexity.

String Quartet No. 4 continues along the lines of sound exploration seen in *Strata* and *String Quartet No. 3*, in which a change of sound is used as a method of developing a pitch and traditional musical sounds are developed by non-traditional methods, for example, scratching or slapping the strings or the instrument. They incorporate non-traditional sounds to augment the traditional methods of dealing with material. *String Quartet No. 4* has only a single movement, divided into four parts – or more correctly four moods – quiet mystery; a more active section with a suggestion of bird sounds; an alternation of rhythmic with non-rhythmic; and a return to the quiet mood of the original section.

Instead of the melodies found in works of her early period, or the sharp motifs of the next period, the essential material of this composition can be described only as: pitch, sound, and activity, as can be seen in Example 7.30. The quartet begins with the note A, and it is upon this single note that the entire composition is based. At the opening the pitch A is passed from instrument to instrument while it is opposed by other pitches, both dissonant (G sharp, B flat), and consonant (E, D). Sound is explored by variations in volume, texture, intensity, and method of production (bowed, plucked, muted, vibrato, and so on). And the element of activity concerns the employment of various rhythms to A and its variants.

The quartet operates on that level of abstract musical ideas, and a description of the work is a description of the pitch, colour, and rhythmic treatment of the note A as it passes from a quiet state at the beginning, is developed by means of variations of all of its sound and time properties, and returns to its original restful state.

In effect, Pentland has reversed the relationship of certain traditional and modern techniques of musical expression since her earliest works based on the Webern-Boulez influence. *Symphony for Ten Parts* has melodic and rhythmic motifs at the basis of the composition, to which were added the new ideas of sound colour. In *Strata* and *String Quartet*

No. 3 the colouristic elements become a more integral part of the composition, sharing their importance with clear melodic and rhythmic motifs. But in *Ēventa* and *String Quartet No. 4* the varied dimensions of sound colour have become the principal elements of the composition, to which melodic and rhythmic motifs appear to be secondary – merely vehicles for the sound exploration.

This new direction or, more correctly, the logical extension of Pentland's experimentation over the last twenty years suggests she may soon discard the last remnants of the serial technique in favour of colour as the major controlling factor. The new devices of quarter-tones and indefinite tones lend their own kind of sound control, and as non-traditional pitch and sound become more and more the essence of her expression, that element may eventually fully replace her present system.

It is exciting to follow Pentland's continual exploration of new sounds and techniques of expression. She continues to do what she has done all her creative life: reflect the most modern elements of her society.

7.29 *Disasters of the Sun*, bars 224–228. See p. 105.

To the Purcell String Quartet: Sydney Humphreys, Bryan King, Philippe Etter & Ian Hampton.

STRING QUARTET 4

Commissioned for the Purcell String Quartet by the Okanagan Summer School of the Arts for its 21st Anniversary (1980)

Barbara Pentland [1979-80]

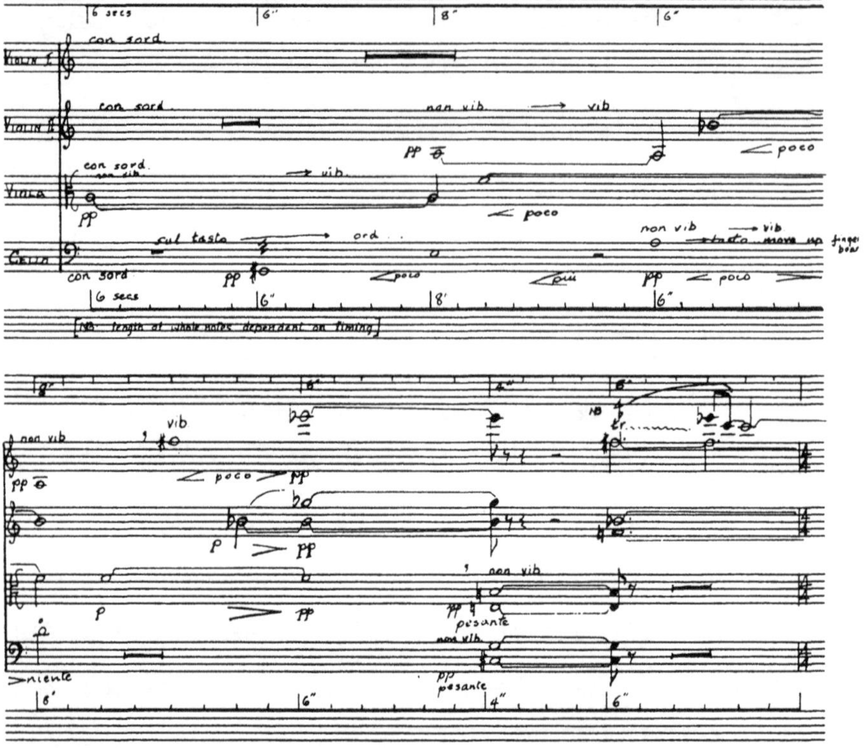

[NB ¼ tone trill]

7.30 *String Quartet No. 4*, pp. 1 and 2. See p. 107.

8.1 *From Long Ago, Flight*, bars 1–3. See p. 109.

THREE PAIRS

I

Day-dreaming

Barbara Pentland

8.2 *Three Pairs, Day-Dreaming*. See p. 110.

8.3 *Echoes I*, bars 1–10. See p. 110.

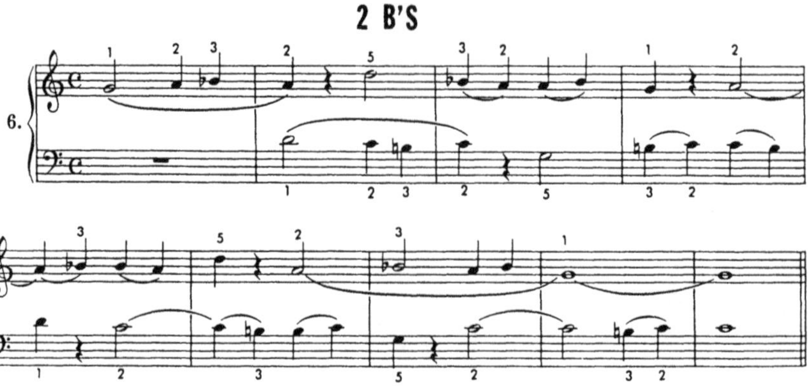

8.4 *Music of Now*, book I, p. 16. See p. 112.

8

Music for beginners

No discussion of Pentland's music would be complete without some mention of her didactic works, the compositions for beginning pianists of all ages, and especially the pieces for the young.

All Pentland's teaching pieces except the most recent are for the piano; the first, in *Six Pieces for Children*, were written in 1938–9, the most recent, *Arctica*, 1971–3. All share some common traits: they are short, in a simple and clear form; the range of intervals is small; and the notes fall easily under the hand. They reflect many of the basic writing techniques Pentland uses in her other compositions: the importance of intervallic relationship, economy of material, and use of short, clear motifs. They differ from her advanced works in that they are less dissonant, the technical demands are intentionally limited, the phrases are more conjunct, and the serial technique is not always used.

Among the earliest of these works, three teaching pieces, under the general title *From Long Ago* (1946), were written while Pentland was teaching at the University Settlement Music School in Toronto and just becoming interested in writing music that would interest pianists with limited technical facility. All three pieces have traits of her early style, and the first in the set, *Lone Traveler*, shows the influence of Copland. The composition is intended to represent the West, a reference in several of Copland's compositions, and Pentland has adopted some of his sounds in her work. The other two pieces have quite different orientations, but still the influence of Copland can be heard. In *Flight*, an Alberti-bass pattern is used but with a modern twist: the four-note pattern calls for an accent every three notes (Example 8.1), thereby adding a modern rhythmic touch and helping the player develop independent finger action. *Obstinate Tune* is built around a simple diatonic melody that keeps recurring within a polytonal setting. The title refers to 'ostinato.' Pentland had decided at that time to give her teaching works colourful programmatic titles, a practice she has continued throughout her career. The titles are attractive, especially to young people, and usually give the performer a clue to the expression. When possible Pentland also includes some programmatic sounds in the composition to assist with the image. *Freedom March* (1963), for example, has drum sounds in the bass and an imitation of trumpet fanfares in the upper range. The march portrays a band that is first heard in the distance, becomes louder as it passes by, and then gradually fades off into the distance.

With the exception of the three-volume *Music of Now* (1969–70), Pentland's teaching pieces are not directed at a single technical level. The element that sets them apart from her other piano compositions is the conscious limitation of technical demands, but even here there is quite a variety. *From Long Ago* is on a fairly simple level, but *Sad Clown* and *Song of Sleep* (both 1949) require a more able pianist. *Sad Clown* includes rapid scale passages, parallel thirds and octaves, and a number of fairly demanding rhythmic passages. *Mirror Study* (1952) also contains running passages, but Pentland has taken special care to keep all double notes well within the hand. In this work the student is introduced to mirror writing in a linear two-voice texture, written so as not to require difficult hand positions.

In most of her compositions for students Pentland is conscious of writing passages that are easily fingered. In the more simple works she simply leaves each hand over the same five notes and writes a piece that is severely limited in range. A good example of this approach is *Three Pairs* (1964), six one-page compositions paired in slow–fast movements based on the same material. In each piece the rhythms are simple and the two-voice texture relies heavily on mirror canon (Example 8.2). Depending on how Pentland has selected the five-finger positions, these six simple compositions vary from tonal to modal to bi-tonal orientation.

A more advanced finger technique is called for in *Echoes I and II* (1964), in which the phrases are written for a fixed five-finger position, but from phrase to phrase the hands shift to a new fixed position. She further limits the demands by requiring only one hand at a time to shift position while the other hand depresses four keys to create sympathetic vibrations (see Example 8.3). Hand shift is also included in *Maze [and] Puzzle* (1968) to the extent that all twelve tones are included.

Serial technique is used in *Signs* (1964), *Freedom March* (1963), *Puppet-Show* (1964), *Songs of Peace and Protest* (1968), *Hands across the C* (1965), and *Space Studies* (1967), demonstrating how that technique can be used with attractive musical results in compositions of limited technical demands. *Puppet-Show* has the added feature of a straightforward presentation of the row, calling the attention of the student to it and giving the teacher a clear example for discussion of serial technique.

Pentland's motive for writing for students was to provide compositions in a modern idiom at a level where the students were forming both their piano technique and their musical tastes. Very little modern music is easily available for beginning musicians, a situation not much different from that for the technically proficient. Most pianists are taught entirely with music from the past. When the training involves the music of creative composers such as Bach, Mozart, Haydn, and Schumann, it is at least artistic material. Unfortunately, the teaching material is more frequently by well-intentioned but musically sterile writers who ape the superficial qualities of the classical masters. But no matter how good is the music of the past, entirely to omit modern music from a musician's training is an unfortunate constriction both technically and musically. It is from this point of view, similar to her concern for the listening public, that Pentland first began to write teaching pieces.

In 1966 Pentland was asked to compose a piano tutor by Rachel Cavalho, a prominent piano teacher in Toronto, who shares Pentland's concern for the place of modern music in teaching. Cavalho has persuaded a number of composers to write for students and further had advocated use of these modern compositions in her lectures and seminars for other teachers. Owing to the effort of Cavalho and others, new works by good Canadian composers now appear regularly on festival programs and conservatory lists, and both teachers and students are becoming acquainted with modern sounds, styles, and techniques.

Cavalho had very definite ideas about the way in which new technical ideas should be presented to students, and Pentland accepted her advice. The combination of talents and mutual respect was a good one: Cavalho knew how to develop technique and interest in young pianists; Pentland could supply the creative compositions; and further, they shared a common concern for young musicians and modern music. The result of their combined efforts is *Music of Now* (1969–70), a three-volume graded approach to piano technique starting from the first introduction to the instrument and written music, and ending with a fairly advanced technique.

The success of *Music of Now* is very much the result of the combined talents of Pentland and Cavalho. For the pace of the books and the sequence of the problems Pentland relied on the experience of Cavalho. In general, the technical approach adopted was of only one technical problem per piece; intervals for one hand not to exceed a sixth; and no more than three chords in a row, given the lack of strength in young fingers. After every few technical advances there is a review of the new achievements and occasionally a composition on a less demanding technical level to offer encouragement and remind the student how much has been accomplished.

Pentland's own experiences in the 1940s teaching young people also are incorporated into the tutor. In her prefatory remarks to book I she suggests that students should be encouraged to feel the shape of the music through gesture and dance movement, and to create their own melodies using the tones of the piece they have just learned. 'Improvising on the given materials should be encouraged throughout.' Singing as well as playing a line is suggested, and rhythms are written out for clapping or tapping.

The approach to piano technique reflects clearly the way in which Pentland approaches composition. Intervals are stressed from the very first page where the difference between whole and half-step is pointed out. Intervallic relationship rather than scales then becomes the foundation of the remainder of the tutor, with mirror phrases the most frequently found device. To stress phrase shape and rhythmic independence, regular bar lines are omitted until half-way through book I, and when they are introduced it is only as a counting aid; by then the student has already been thoroughly grounded in phrases and rhythmic patterns that extend through several bars. Most pieces are linear and contrapuntal, with canon and imitation of various kinds used to make the student aware of line, phrase, and motivic development.

Throughout the three volumes Pentland introduces technical ideas in their modern use rather than the traditional: accidentals are first used as the natural solution to a mirror imitation problem (Example 8.4), rather than in the more traditional form as parts of a scale system; and chords are first found as clusters to be played with the fist, only later to be individually fingered. No key signatures are used, although accidentals are found frequently, and by book III the students have been exposed to a number of contemporary devices in addition to tone clusters, such as retrograde melodic writing, widely spaced sounds within a single phrase, changing metre, irregular metres (5/4, 5/8), and shifting rhythmic organization within regular metres.

With the training provided in *Music of Now* students are equipped to handle music of any era including that of the present. The stress on phrasing, clarity of rhythm, and the linear aspects of music makes a good background for any keyboard repertory, and the encouragement to improvise helps the pianist to begin to think from the point of view of the composer. *Music of Now* is a well-thought-out approach to learning piano. It is thorough, innovative, and creative, and the pieces are attractive. Pentland has the uncommon ability to realize what musical things appeal to young people and the corresponding talent to compose on that level.

After *Music of Now* Pentland branched out to include student works for other instruments: *Reflections/Reflets* (1971) for free-bass accordion, *Five-Plus* (1971) for string orchestra, and *Phases for Solo Clarinet* (1977). In 1979 she composed *Variable Winds*, a set of four short pieces that can be played on a number of different wind instruments. The title is a typical Pentland play on words, and she carries the idea further by naming the individual pieces *Sirocco*, *Nor'-easter*, *Squalls*, and *Zephyr*. Each piece is a musical representation of the wind named in its title. *Variable Winds* can be performed by a number of different wind instruments, either as unaccompanied solo or as a duet with an optional percussion part. The pieces are based on intervals rather than a tone row and have varying amounts of modern compositional devices. *Sirocco* and *Nor'-easter* demand only traditional notes and rhythms; *Squalls* has an aleatoric zone within it; and *Zephyr* calls for variable pitch, flutter-tongue, quarter-tones, and glissando. The new techniques are all carefully explained in the preface, and there are four different versions, transposed in order to place the notes within the range of different instruments. The pieces are fun and the technical demands are within the limitations of most good secondary school musicians. *Variable Winds* is a welcome addition to a very small repertory of modern music written with intermediate players in mind.

Epilogue

As stated in the preface, we did not set out to analyse or describe all of Pentland's compositions. Her works are so many and so different from one another that it has not been possible to discuss all the different varieties, and it is left to the listener and performer to discover the many works of quality passed over here for lack of space. A few highlights are *Toccata* (1958), modelled on similar works by the seventeenth-century composer Girolamo Frescobaldi; the almost impressionistic *Three Duets after Pictures by Paul Klee* (1958–9); the two works for accordion, *Reflections / Reflets* (1971) and *Interplay for Free-Bass Accordion and String Quartet* (1972); and *Trance* (1978), for flute and piano or harp. The scores can be borrowed from the Canadian Music Centre.

In spite of occasional physical disabilities in the past few years, Pentland gives no indication of slowing down. The number of works produced in the 1970s is somewhat less than before, but it includes *News* and *Disasters of the Sun*, her most dramatic large-scale compositions; an impressive variety of smaller works; and her more recent ventures into sound contrasts, in *Ēventa* and *String Quartet No. 4*. As recently as October 1978 she joined Robert Rogers in a performance of *Duets after Pictures by Paul Klee* during his recital of her piano compositions in the UBC Recital Hall, her first public appearance in eleven years.

Her interest in the constantly changing techniques of composition continues. She investigates new ideas and explores new sounds for each new composition. In 1971 and 1972 she wrote music for the free-bass accordion, an instrument she had not used before, and when she was commissioned in 1977 by Contemporary Showcase in Toronto to write *Phases for Solo Clarinet* she accepted and then took a clarinet lesson in order to understand better the possibilities and limitations of the instrument.

She has followed with great interest the developments in electronic music, but as yet has not attempted it herself. When asked about it she often cites the most practical reason – the lack of available equipment – although that type of limitation has never stopped her in the past. She also has said that she feels a need to write out her music on five lines – she likes the look of the notes. But her most recent experiments with colouristic devices and modern sound techniques are in the direction of the flexibility more easily achieved by electronics, and an electronic composition by her in the near future is certainly a possibility.

Her 1963 retirement from teaching left more time to pursue her wide range of interests such as reading, bird watching, and politics. On doctor's orders she travels south to escape Vancouver's dampness in winter. She became interested in undersea life in 1965, and her husband designed an undersea face mask with her eyeglass prescription built in so the two of them could enjoy snorkeling in places such as Hawaii, Maui, Grand Cayman, and Yucatan. Somehow even this leisure pursuit finds its way into her music as the subject matter of the Ephemera compositions: *Coral Reef* (1974); *Angelus, Spectra*, and *Whales* (all 1977); and *Persiflage* (1978).

Performances, honours, and recognition of her work, both in Canada and abroad, have finally begun to take place regularly – at a time when she no longer feels the same need she once did for assurances that she is headed in the right direction. During the 1960s and 1970s a number of CBC programs have featured her works. In 1967 the University of Saskatchewan presented a series of concerts of her works together with a display of her music and lectures to the music classes. She was given the Diplôme d'Honneur in 1977 by the Canadian Conference of the Arts for distinguished service to the arts in Canada. In 1976 the Swedish Broadcasting Corporation devoted an entire program to her music. She has had seventeen of her works recorded (see Appendix B) and regularly receives commissions for compositions; an exceptionally pleasing recent commission was *Ēventa* (1978) for the New Music Concerto Series, in Toronto, from her former student Robert Aitken, an internationally known flutist who also toured Europe in 1979 with *Trance* (1978).

The recent press reviews of her works more often than not show that the critics and audience are becoming more accustomed to modern sounds. There are still some bitter remarks from time to time, such as the comparison of her *String Quartet No. 3* to the sound-track for a headache remedy (Victoria *Daily Colonist* 20 Feb 1971), and she still cringes over the interview by a female writer that ignored her music and concentrated on her appearance (Winnipeg *Tribune* 25 Feb 1960). But in general the wishes expressed in her writings of the 1940s and 1950s have begun to be fulfilled: that the audience make an effort to become acquainted with modern music.

She has accomplished a great deal through her single-minded devotion to her art. She is very much an artist of her century, living fully in a world she has helped to shape, and it is hoped that this review of her works will encourage more performers and listeners to explore the many moods, skilful craftsmanship, and high musical artistry of Barbara Pentland.

APPENDIX A

Compositions

Entries provide the following information, where applicable: title (text), instrumentation, publisher, duration, and first performance (performers).

?

Book of Early Pieces (destroyed)

1921

The Blue Grotto; pno; ms

1922

Twilight; pno; ms

1923

Dawn; pno; ms

Berceuse; pno; ms

That Darling Old Dad O'Mine; ms

1924–9

Revolutionary Sonata (Fantasia) (unfinished); pno; ms

1929

The Cottager to Her Infant; voice and pno; ms

Bergers et vous, Bergères; unaccompanied chorus SATB, voice and pno; ms

---

1930

Sonate in C sharp minor; pno; ms. Dedication: 'À mon cher Professeur Madame Gauthiez hommage respectueux'

Trio for Flute, Cello and Piano; fl, vcl, pno; ms

Aveu fleuri; voice and pno; ms

Numerous motets with and without organ accompaniment; ms

1931

Rêverie; pno; ms

1932

Sonatine; pno; ms

Piece in B Minor; pno; ms

A Lavender Lady (George H. Clarke); voice and pno; ms.
Winnipeg, Sept 1936 (A. Kelsey, sop; A. Hovey, pno)

Ruins (Ypres, 1917) (George H. Clarke); voice and pno; ms.
Winnipeg, Sept 1936 (A. Kelsey, sop; A. Hovey, pno)

1933

Pastorale; pno; ms

1934

Lament (Wilfred Wilson Gibson); voice, string quartet; ms

1935

Invocation; vln, pno; ms

Two Preludes; pno; ms.
Winnipeg, Sept 1936 (composer)

They Are Not Long (Ernest Dawson); voice and pno; ms.
Winnipeg, Sept 1936 (A. Kelsey, sop; A. Hovey, pno)

Concert-Overture; sym orch; ms

1936

Sonata; pno; ms.
1st mvt: Winnipeg, Sept 1936 (composer)

1937

Academic Allegro; vln, pno; ms

Mazurka; pno; ms.
Winnipeg, Oct 1938 (S. Sigurdson)

Starless Night; voice and pno; ms

Little Scherzo for Clavichord; clavichord; ms.
Winnipeg, Oct 1938 (S. Sigurdson)

Ballad of the Trees and the Master (Sidney Lanier); chorus, SATB; ms.
Winnipeg, Oct 1938 (F. Hubble, cond)

Prelude, Chorale and Toccata; organ; ms.
New York, May 1938 (A. Miller)

1938

Two Pieces for Strings; string orch; ms

Leisure (W.H. Davies); chorus, SAT; ms.
Winnipeg, March 1939 (F. Hubble, cond)

A Picture (anon); chorus, SAT; ms.
Winnipeg, March 1939 (F. Hubble, cond)

Cradle Song (Padraic Colum); chorus, SATB; ms.
Winnipeg, March 1939 (F. Hubble, cond)

A Piper (Seamas O'Sullivan); chorus, SATB; ms

Ostinato; organ; ms

Sonata Allegro; pno; ms

The Mask (W.H. Davies); voice and pno; ms

Elegy; pno; ms

Five Preludes
1 *Prologue*

2 *Legend*
3 *Jest*
4 *Romance*
5 *Curtain*
piano; ms.
8′; titled *Suite of 4 Pieces*: Winnipeg, March 1939 (S. Sigurdson); titled *Five Preludes*: New York, April 1939 (E. Voorhies)

1939

Six Pieces for Children; pno; ms

Piano Quartet; pno, vln, vla, vcl; ms.
20′; Winnipeg, March 1941 (composer, pno; M. Gussin, vln; M. Graham, vla; B. Schmidt, vcl)

Lament; sym orch; ms.
7′; Winnipeg, Aug 1940 (Winnipeg Summer Sym, G. Waddington, cond)

Dirge for a Violet (Duncan Campbell Scott); unaccompanied chorus, SATB; ms

Rhapsody 1939: The World on the March to War Again; pno; ms.
5′30″; Winnipeg, March 1941 (composer)

The Devil Dances; cl, pno; ms

1940

Unvanquished (Dallas Kenmare); tenor, pno; ms

Promenade in Mauve; pno; ms

Fantasy for Piano and Orchestra (unfinished); ms

Payload (score for a radio drama; Anne Marriott); ms.
Montreal, Nov 1940 (CBC Sym, J.M. Beaudet, cond)

Beauty and the Beast (ballet-pantomine); two pno; ms.
Winnipeg, Jan 1941 (composer and M. Dillabough)

1941

The Wind Our Enemy (score for a radio drama; Anne Marriott); ms

Arioso and Rondo (originally *Little Symphony for Full Orchestra*); sym orch; ms.
10′; *Rondo*: Toronto, Jan 1942 (CBC Orch, S. Hersenhoren, cond); complete: London, July 1945 (BBC Sym, A. Boult, cond)

Studies in Line; pno; BMI Canada Ltd 1949.
5′50″; Winnipeg, Dec 1941 (M. Dillabough)

Holiday Suite; cham orch; ms.
10′; Vancouver, July 1948 (CBC Chamber Orch, J. Avison, cond)

1942

Variations for Piano; pno; ms.
7′; Winnipeg, March 1942 (composer)

Concerto for Violin and Small Orchestra; solo vln, 2 cl, 2 hrn, vln, vla, vcl, db; ms.
17′; Toronto, Jan 1945 (H. Adaskin, vln; F. Marr, pno)

1943

Payload (Suite for Orchestra); orch; ms.
CBC 'Music for Radio,' Jan 1943

Sonata for Cello and Piano; vcl, pno; ms.
15′; finale: Montreal, Sept 1946 (L. Brott, vcl; N. Chotem, pno); complete: Vancouver, Mar 1950 (B. Frank, vcl; composer, pno)

1944

Air-Bridge to Asia; (radio drama); ms.
CBC, Nov 1944 (S. Hersenhoren, cond)

1942–5

Song Cycle (Anne Marriott)
1 *Wheat*
2 *Forest*
3 *Tracks*
4 *Mountains*
5 *Cities*
sop, pno; ms.
11′; *Tracks*: Toronto, Dec 1944 (F. James, sop; composer, pno); complete: Toronto, April 1947 (F. James, sop; composer, pno)

1944–5

String Quartet No. 1; 2 vln, vla, vcl; ms.
14′; Philadelphia, April 1949 (D. Steiner and N. Heaton, vlns; S. Cossum, vla; J. Eppinoff, vcl)

1945

At Early Dawn (Hsiang Hao); tenor, fl, vcl; ms

Piano Sonata; pno; ms.
14′; Prague, July 1947 (M. Knotkova)

Vista; vln, pno; BMI Canada Ltd 1951.
9′; Vancouver, Aug 1948 (H. Adaskin, vln; F. Marr, pno)

1946

Sonata for Violin and Piano; vln, pno; ms.
15′; Winnipeg, May 1948 (I. Thorolfson, vln; C. Duncan, pno)

From Long Ago
1 *Lone Traveler*
2 *Obstinate Tune*
3 *Flight*
pno; ms (*Lone Traveller*: RCMT Grade VIII book, Frederick Harris 1978)

1947

Sonata Fantasy; pno; ms.
13′; Toronto, March 1948 (H. Somers)

Holiday Suite (string version); string orch; ms.
Toronto, June 1947 (CBC Sym Strings, H. Sumberg, cond)

Colony Music: Overture, Chorale, Burlesque; pno, string orch; ms.
12′; Toronto, Feb 1948 (New World Orch, S. Hersenhoren, cond); commissioned by Forest Hill Community Centre

The Living Gallery (score for National Film Board); ms.
Mexico City, Nov 1947

1945–8

Symphony No. 1; picc 222 bs cl 2: 4331: timp, perc, hp, strgs; ms.
25′; Adagio: Montreal, Oct 1947 (CBC Orch, A. Brott, cond)

1948

Variations on a Boccherini Tune; fl, ob, hrn, strings; ms.
11′30″; Toronto, June 1948 (CBC Orch, S. Hersenhoren, cond); commissioned by the CBC

Octet for Winds; fl, ob, B flat cl, bsn, B flat trpt, horn I and II, trb; ms.
8′; Toronto, Jan 1949 (Toronto Sym Wind Players, H. Sumberg, cond)

Dirge; pno; BMI Canada Ltd 1961.
3′30″; Seattle, Jan 1953 (composer)

1949

Sad Clown, Song of Sleep; pno; ms

Weekend Overture for resort combo; cl, trpt, pno, perc; ms

Concerto for Organ and Strings; org, string orch; ms.
14'25"; London, April 1951 (G. Jeffery, org; London Chamber Orch, E. White, cond); commissioned by Jeffery and White

---

1950

Solo Violin Sonata; vln; ms.
17'; Brussels, June 1955 (L. Thienpont)

Cadenzas for Mozart Violin Concerto, K207; vln; ms.
Vancouver, 1950 (H. Adaskin, vln)

Symphony No. 2; 2122: 2220: timp, perc, stgs; ms.
16'; 1st mvt: Vancouver, Nov 1952 (Vancouver Junior Sym, C. Slim, cond); complete: Toronto, Feb 1953 (CBC Sym, E. Mazzoleni, cond); commissioned by the Youth Music League for the Vancouver Junior Sym Orch

---

1951

Ave atque vale; picc II cor ang II cfg: 2331: timp, perc, stgs; ms.
7'30"; Vancouver, Nov 1953 (Vancouver Sym Orch, I. Hoffman, cond); 'In mem. B.W. d. 1951'

Sonatina No. 1; pno; ms.
8'; Vancouver, April 1954 (composer)

Sonatina No. 2; pno; ms.
6'40"; Seattle, Jan 1953 (composer)

1952

Epigrams and Epitaphs; 2, 3, and 4 voc, unaccompanied; ms

Mirror Study; pno; ms.
1'

The Lake (one-act chamber opera; Dorothy Livesay); sop; contr; ten; bass; fl; ob; B flat trpt, vln I (3); vln II (3); vla (2); vcl (2); db; ms.
27'; Vancouver, Mar 1954 (Minunzie, Nowell, Cole, Fyfe, singers; CBC Chamber Orch, J. Avison, cond)

1953

String Quartet No. 2; vln I and II; vla; vcl; ms.
26'; Stockholm, June 1956 (Grunfarb Quartet); 'In mem. Charles H. Pentland'

Two-Piano Sonata; two pno; CMC.
10'; Cambridge, Mass, May 1954 (E. Arrow, C. Slim); 'Colin Slim'

1954

Aria; pno; ms.
2'45"; Vancouver, Feb 1955 (composer)

What Is Man? (Ecclesiasticus XVIII); chorus, SATB; ms

Salutation of the Dawn (Sanskrit); chorus, SATB; ms

Sonatina for Solo Flute; fl; ms.
6'; Vancouver, Feb 1955 (J. Murphy)

1955

Ricercar for Strings; string orch; ms.
5'05"; Vancouver, Aug 1958 (CBC Chamber Orch, N. Goldschmidt, cond)

Interlude; pno; Waterloo Music Co Ltd 1968.
2'10"; Vancouver, Feb 1956 (composer)

1955–6

Concerto for Piano and Strings; pno; string orch; ms.
15'15"; Toronto, Mar 1958 (M. Bernardi, pno; CBC Sym, V. Feldbrill, cond)

1957

Symphony for Ten Parts (No. 3); fl; ob; F hrn; C trpt; xyl; timp; vln; vla; vcl; db; BMI Canada Ltd 1961.
10'; Vancouver, CBC, Sept 1959 (H. McLean, cond)

1958

Toccata; pno; BMI Canada Ltd 1961.
8'05"; Vancouver, July 1958 (composer)

1958–9

Three Duets after Pictures by Paul Klee
1 *Small Fool in Trance*
2 *Surfaces in Tension*
3 *Fish Magic*
pno, 4 hands; ms.
6'15"; Vancouver, Feb 1961 (composer; R. Rogers)

1959

Symphony No. 4; 2222: 4331: timp, perc, stgs; ms.
20'; Winnipeg, Feb 1960 (Winnipeg Sym Orch, V. Feldbrill, cond); commissioned by the Winnipeg Sym Orch on a grant from the Canada Council; dedication: John Huberman

---

1960

Duo for Viola and Piano; vla; pno; ms.
17'; Vancouver, Nov. 1960 (H. Adaskin, vla; F. Marr, pno)

1961

Canzona for Flute, Oboe and Harpsichord; fl; ob; hpschd; ms.
6'; Montreal, Oct 1962 (Baroque Trio of Montreal: M. Duschenes, fl; M. Berman, ob; K. Jones, hpschd)

Cavazzoni for Brass (three organ hymns of Girolamo Cavazzoni transcribed for quintet); tpt I and II; F hrn; tbn; tuba; ms.
Vancouver, Feb 1966 (Vancouver Brass Ensemble)

1961–2

Ostinato and Dance for Harpsichord; hpschd; ms.
4'15"

1962

Fantasy; pno; BMI Canada Ltd 1966.
6'40"; Vancouver, Feb 1963 (L. Stein)

1963

Trio for Violin, Cello and Piano; vln; vcl; pno; ms.
12′; Feb 1964 (Halifax Trio: F. Chaplin, vln; E. Bisha, vlc; G. Macpherson, pno); commissioned by the CBC for the Halifax Trio; 'To my Father, in Memoriam'

Freedom March; pno, 4 hands; ms.
1′20″

Two Canadian Folk-Songs
1 *Je le mène bien, mon dévidoir*
2 *À la claire fontaine*
pno, 4 hands; ms

1964

Signs (Four Easy Pieces for Piano)
1 *Angles*
2 *Curves*
3 *Dashes*
4 *Dots*
pno; ms

Three Pairs
1 *Day-Dreaming/Turn about*
2 *Reflection/Follow Me!*
3 *Slow Song/Folk Dance*
pno; BMI Canada Ltd 1966

Puppet-Show; pno, 4 hands; BMI Canada Ltd 1966.
4′50″

Echoes I and II; pno; Waterloo Music Co Ltd 1968

Shadows – Ombres; pno; Waterloo Music Co Ltd 1968
4′15″; Vancouver, June 1965 (composer)

Puzzle; pno; with *Maze* 1968

Sung Songs 1–3 (trans Clara M. Handlin)
1 *Divining* (Huang T'ing Chien)
2 *Life* (Hsin Ch'i Chi)
3 *Let the Harp Speak* (Yen Chi-tao)
voice and pno; ms.
7′30″; Vancouver CBC, April 1968 (W. Denyes, sop; H. Brown, pno)

Strata; string orch; ms.
9′30″; Vancouver, Sept 1968 (CBC Chamber Orch, J. Avison, cond)

1964–5

Three Sung Songs (trans Clara M. Handlin)
1 *Wanderer's Woe* (Li Yu)
2 *I Daily Look for You* (Liu Yung)
3 *Spring Days Come Suddenly* (Ch'eng Hao)
chorus, SATB; ms.
Spring Days: Montreal, Sept 1967 (Le Petit Ensemble Vocal, G. Little, cond)

1965

Caprice; pno; ms.
2′20″; Vancouver, Feb 1966 (composer)

Hands across the C
1 *Sparks*
2 *Mist*
3 *Seashore*
pno; Waterloo Music Co Ltd 1968

Variations for Viola; vla; ms.
11′; Burnaby, BC, 1975 (S. Wilkes)

1966

Trio con alea; vln; vla; vcl; ms.
25′; Vancouver, Feb 1967 (J. Loban, vln; H.-K. Piltz, vla; E.Wilson, vcl; commissioned by the UBC Dept of Music Chamber Music Ensemble, with the collaboration of the CMC under a grant from the Centennial Commission

Suite Borealis
1 *Unknown Shores*
2 *Settlements*
3 *Rapids*
4 *Wide Horizons*
5 *Mountains*
pno; ms.
20′; Vancouver, March 1967 (C. Jutte: *Unknown Shores, Rapids*; G. Carey: *Settlements*; W. Renard: *Wide Horizons*; R. Kitson: *Mountains*); commissioned by the ARCT Association of Vancouver

---

1967

Septet; F hrn; C trpt; trbn; org; vln; vla; vcl; ms.
14′; Vancouver, Feb 1968 (H. McLean, org; K. Hopkins, trpt; R. Creech, hrn; I. McDougall, trbn; C. Trowsdale, vln; S. Humphreys, vla; I. Hampton, vcl); commissioned by the Hugh McLean Consort with the collaboration of the CMC

Space Studies
1 *Frolic*
2 *From Outer Space*
3 *Quest*
4 *Balancing Act*
pno; Waterloo Music Co Ltd 1968

1968

Songs of Peace and Protest; pno; ms

Maze/Labyrinthe, Casse-Tête/Puzzle; pno; Waterloo Music Co Ltd 1969

Cinéscene; 1111: 1111: timp, perc, stgs; ms.
8′

1969

Music of Now, Book I; pno; Waterloo Music Co Ltd 1970

Music of Now, Book II; pno; Waterloo Music Co Ltd 1970

String Quartet No. 3; vln I and II; vla; vcl; ms.
23′50″; Vancouver, June 1970 (Purcell String Quartet: N. Nelson, R. Owens, vlns; P. Etter, vla; I. Hampton, vcl); commissioned by the Purcell String Quartet; dedication: Purcell String Quartet

---

1970

Music of Now, Book III; pno; Waterloo Music Co Ltd 1970

News (extracts from news media); virtuoso voice, 2022: 2120: perc, pno, stgs, tape recorder; ms.
26′; Ottawa, July 1971 (P. Mailing, sop; National Arts Centre Orch, M. Bernardi, cond); commissioned by the CBC

Variations concertantes; solo pno, 1110: 1110: perc, stgs; ms.
8′; Montreal, June 1971 (Z. Shaulis, pno; Montreal Sym Orch, F.-P. Decker, cond); commissioned by L'Institut International de musique du Canada (test piece)

1971

Five-Plus (transcription of *Songs of Peace and Protest*, 1968); string orch; ms.
5′50″

Reflections/Reflets; free-bass accordion; ms.
5′; Vancouver, 1973 (L. Thiessen)

Sung Songs Nos. 4 and 5 (trans Clara M. Handlin)
4 *Midnight among the Hills* (H'Sin Ch'i-chi)
5 *The Tune of the Stream* (H'Sin Ch'i Chi)

medium voice and pno; CMC.
8'; Vancouver, Nov 1972 (P. Mailing, mezzo-sop; D. Bampton, pno)

1972

Interplay for Free-Bass Accordion and String Quartet; free-bass accordion; string quartet; ms.
13'; Vancouver, May 1974 (J. Macerollo, acc; Purcell String Quartet); commissioned by the CBC for Macerollo

Mutations; vcl; pno; ms.
18'; Vancouver, Feb 1973 (E. Wilson, vcl; R. Rogers, pno); commissioned by the CBC for Wilson and Rogers

---

1971–3

Arctica
1 *Ice Floe*
2 *Thaw*
3 *Snowy Owl*
4 *Tuktu*
pno; CMC.
Toronto 1974 (Contemporary Showcase)

1973

Vita brevis; pno; CMC.
5'; Vancouver, Oct 1978 (R. Rogers); 'To J.H.'

1974

Occasions
1 *Fanfare*
2 *Cortège*
3 *Fiesta*
C trpt I and II; F hrn; trbn; tuba; ms.
9'; Vancouver, Aug 1974 (Vancouver Brass Quintet); commissioned by the CBC for the Vancouver Brass Quintet

Coral Reef (later included as Ephemera 4); pno; ms.
2'30"; Vancouver, Oct 1978

1975

Res musica; vln I (4); vln II (4); vla (3); vcl (2); db; ms.
15'; Vancouver, May 1975 (Baroque Strings of Vancouver, N. Nelson cond); commissioned by the Baroque Strings of Vancouver (through a grant from Mrs Caroline Riley)

1976

Disasters of the Sun (Dorothy Livesay); mezzo-sop; fl; B flat cl; horn; 2 perc; pno; tape recorder; vln; vla; vcl; ms.
30'; Vancouver, Jan 1977 (P. Mailing); commissioned by the Vancouver New Music Society

Tenebrae; pno; ms.
8'; Vancouver, Oct 1978 (R. Rogers)

1977

The Lake (revised version); sop; contr; ten; bass; fl; ob; B flat trpt; pno; vln I and II; vla; vcl; ms.
27'

Phases for Solo Clarinet; B flat clarinet; ms.
Under 10'; Toronto, Feb 1978 (D. Constant); commissioned by Contemporary Showcase

Angelus, Spectra, Whales (Ephemera 1, 2, and 3); pno; ms.
1: 4'; 2: 2'30"; 3: 1'30"; Vancouver, Oct 1978 (R. Rogers)

1978

Persiflage (Ephemera 5); pno; ms.
Vancouver, Oct 1978 (R. Rogers)

Trance; fl; pno or harp; ms.
Toronto, Jan 1979 (E. Goodman; R. Aitken)

Ēventa; fl; cl; trbn; vln; vcl; hrp; perc; ms.
15′; Toronto, April 1979 (R. Aitken, fl and cond); commissioned by New Music Concerts

---

1979

Variable Winds
1 *Sirocco*; fl or ob; alt sax; cor ang
2 *Nor'easter*; cl; hrn
3 *Squalls*; bsn; tba or euph
4 *Zephyr*; trbn; bass cl; optional perc
ms.
5′

Ballad for Soprano and Violin; voice; vln; ms.
4′

1980

String Quartet No. 4; vln I and II; vla; vcl; ms.
15′; Penticton, BC, July 1980 (Purcell Quartet); commissioned by the Okanagan Summer School of the Arts for its 21st anniversary, for the Purcell Quartet

APPENDIX B

Discography

Concerto for Piano and Strings (1955–6). RCI 184
Mario Bernardi, pno; CBC Symphony Orchestra, Victor Feldbrill, cond

Duo for Viola and Piano (1960). RCA CC/CCS 1017; RCI 223
Smyth Humphreys, vla; Hugh McLean, pno

Echoes I and II (1964). CCM-2
Rachel Cavalho, pno

Fantasy (1962). RCI 242
Barbara Pentland, pno

Hands across the C (1965). CCM-2
Rachel Cavalho, pno

Interplay (1972). Melbourne SMLP 4034
Joseph Macerollo, accordion; Purcell String Quartet

Shadows – Ombres (1964). RCI 242
Barbara Pentland, pno

Space Studies (1967). CCM-2
Rachel Cavalho, pno

String Quartet No. 1 (1944–5). Col ML 5764
Canadian String Quartet

String Quartet No. 1. RCI 141
Montreal String Quartet

String Quartet No. 3 (1969). RCI 353
Purcell String Quartet

Studies in Line (1941). RCI 134
John Newmark, pno

Studies in Line. CCM-2
Rachel Cavalho, pno

Studies in Line. Lon. T. 5697
Reginald Godden, pno

Studies in Line. RCI 496
Angela Hewitt, pno

Suite Borealis (1966). Melbourne SMLP 4031
Antonin Kubalek, pno

Symphony for Ten Parts (No. 3) (1957). RCA CCS 1009; RCI 215/215-S
Chamber Ensemble of the Winnipeg Symphony Orchestra, Victor Feldbrill, cond

Three Duets after Pictures by Paul Klee (1958–9). RCI 242
Barbara Pentland, Robert Rogers, pno

Three Pairs (1964). CCM-2
Rachel Cavalho, pno

Toccata (1958). RCI 242
Barbara Pentland, pno

Toccata. CBC BR SM-162
Walter Buczynski, pno

Trio for Violin, Cello and Piano (1963). RCI 242
Barbara Pentland, pno; Arthur Polson, vln; James Hunter, vcl

Bibliography

BOOKS, ARTICLES, AND THESES

Apel, Paul Hermann *Music of the Americas, North and South* New York 1958

'Barbara Pentland: A Portrait' *Musicanada* XXI (July–Aug 1969) 8–9

'Barbara Pentland' pamphlet, BMI Canada Ltd, 1974

Basham, Leonard 'Canadian Symphonic Composers: The Music of Barbara Pentland' *The Composer* (Aug 1944)

Beckwith, John 'Music' Malcolm Ross ed *The Arts in Canada: A Stocktaking at Mid-Century* Toronto 1958

– 'The Performing Arts' John T. Saywell ed *Canadian Annual Review for 1968* Toronto 1963

– 'What Every U.S. Musician Should Know About Canadian Music' *Musicanada* XXIX (final issue) 7, 13

Berry, Wallace 'Review' *Music Library Association Notes* (Sept 1962) 701

Cadzow, Dorothy 'Music by Canadians' *International Musician* (March 1950) 12

Canadian Fiction Magazine XXX–XXXI (1979) 115

Canadian Music Library Association *A Bio-Bibliographical Finding List of Canadian Musicians and Those Who Have Contributed to Music in Canada* Ottawa 1967

Canadian Radio and Television Annual Toronto 1950, 207

Cavalho, Rachel 'Canadian Piano Music for Teaching' *Musicanada* (June–July and Aug–Sept 1968)

Composers of the Americas VI, Washington, DC, 88–94

'Contemporary Canadian Music for Young Pianists' *Les Cahiers canadiens de musique/Canada Music Book* (spring–summer 1970) 175

Creative Canada I 245–6

Desautels, Andrée 'Canadian Composition' Arnold Walter ed *Aspects of Music in Canada* Toronto 1969
Duncan, Chester 'New Music' *Canadian Music Journal* VI no. 4 (summer 1962) 47
Eastman, Sheila 'Barbara Pentland' *Contemporary Canadian Composers* ed K. MacMillan and J. Beckwith, Toronto 1975
– (under Loosley, Sheila Eastman) 'Barbara Pentland: A Biography' MMus thesis, University of British Columbia 1974
Fuller, Donald 'League of Composers' Concert' *Modern Music* (winter–spring 1942) 177
Gillespie, John *Five Centuries of Keyboard Music* Belmont, Calif, 1965
Gillmor, Alan 'Contemporary Music in Canada – I' *Contact* no. 11 (summer 1975) 6–8
Grobin, Michael 'Our Composers on Microgroove' *Performing Arts in Canada* (spring 1973) 38, 39
Howell, Gordon P. 'The Development of Music in Canada' PhD dissertation, University of Rochester, 1959
Huse, Peter 'Barbara Pentland' *Music Scene* (July–Aug 1968) 9
International Service of the CBC *Thirty-four Biographies of Canadian Composers* Montreal 1964
Johnston, Richard 'Review' *Music across Canada* (Feb 1963) 17
Kallmann, Helmut *A History of Music in Canada 1534–1914* Toronto 1960
– 'Musical Composition in Canada from 1867' *Musicanada* (June 1969) 9
Kasamets, Udo 'New Music' *Canadian Music Journal* VI no. 3 (spring 1962) 43
MacMillan, Sir Ernest *Music in Canada* Toronto 1955
Mitchell, Donald 'Instrumental' *Musical Times* XCVI (Sept 1955) 485
Owen, Stephanie Olive 'The Piano Concerto in Canada since 1955 PhD dissertation, Washington University 1969
Park, Julian, ed *The Culture of Contemporary Canada* Ithaca, NY, 1957
Pentland, Barbara 'On Becoming a Composer' *C.F.T.M.A. Newsletter* (Feb 1976) 10–11
– 'Canadian Music, 1950' *Northern Review* III (Feb–March 1950) 43–6
– 'Dear Sir' (letter to the editor) *C.B.C. Times* (24–30 Aug 1963) 2
– 'On Experiment in Music' *Canadian Review of Music and Art* (Aug–Sept 1943) 25–7
– Letter to the editor *Canadian Music Journal* VI no. 2 (winter 1962) 80
– 'Letters: Comment from a Composer' (letter to the editor) *Musical America* LXXXIII no. 4 (Nov 1963) 4
– 'Looking Ahead' *C.F.T.M.A. Newsletter* (July 1976) 2
– 'Music Publishing in Canada: A Discussion' *Royal Conservatory of Music of Toronto Monthly Bulletin* (Oct 1948) 2

– 'Wanted, An Audience' in a program for a performance by the Jewish Folk Choir in Toronto, 25 March 1947
'Piano Music of the Americas' *Music Journal Anthology Annual* (1963) 81
Proctor, George *Canadian Music of the Twentieth Century* Toronto 1980
Toomey, Kathleen M., and Stephen C. Willis ed *Musicians in Canada: A Bio-Bibliographical Finding List/Musiciens au Canada: Index bio-bibliographique* Ottawa 1981
Turner, Robert 'Barbara Pentland' *Canadian Music Journal* II no. 4 (summer 1958) 15–26
Walter, Arnold 'Canadian Composition' *Music Teachers' National Association Proceedings* XL (1946) 87–105
Wheeler, T. J. ed *Canadian Radio and Television Annual* Toronto 1950

DICTIONARIES AND ENCYCLOPAEDIAS

Carlson, Effie B. *A Bio-Bibliographical Dictionary of 12 Tone and Serial Composers* Metuchen, NJ, 1970
Eastman, Sheila 'Barbara Pentland' Stanley Sadie ed *The New Grove Dictionary of Music and Musicians* London: Vol. 14 1980
Gatti, Guido M., ed *Enciclopedia Della Musica* Milan 1964
Kallmann, Helmut 'Barbara Pentland' Friedrich Blume ed *Die Musik in Geschichte und Gegenwart* Kassel: Vol. 10, 1962
Riemann Musik Lexikon II, Mainz, in press
Slonimsky, Nicholas *Baker's Biographical Dictionary of Musicians* sixth edn, New York 1979
Tonkunstler-Lexikon Wilhelmshaven, in press
Vinton, John, ed *Dictionary of Contemporary Music* New York 1975
Winters, Kenneth 'Barbara Pentland' *Encyclopedia of Music in Canada* Toronto 1981

CATALOGUES

B.M.I. Symphonic Catalogue New York 1971
Catalogue of Canadian Chamber Music Toronto 1967
Catalogue of Canadian Choral Music Toronto 1966
Catalogue of Canadian Composers second edn, Toronto 1952
Catalogue of Canadian Keyboard Music Toronto 1972
Catalogue of Microfilms of Unpublished Canadian Music Toronto 1970
Catalogue of Orchestral Music Toronto 1957
Catalogue of Orchestral Music at the Canadian Music Centre Toronto 1963
List of Canadian Orchestral Music Toronto 1968
Napier, Ronald *A Guide to Canada's Composers* Willowdale 1973

Index

Numbers in italics indicate a discussion of a work; those in bold signify an analysis of a work. Numbers in parentheses indicate a musical example associated with a discussion or analysis.

CANADIAN COMPOSERS SERIES

1 *Harry Somers* by Brian Cherney; Toronto, University of Toronto Press 1975
2 *Jean Papineau-Couture* par Louise Bail-Milot; Montréal, Les Éditions Fides (à paraître)
3 *Barbara Pentland* by Sheila Eastman and Timothy J. McGee; Toronto, University of Toronto Press 1983
4 *R. Murray Schafer* by Stephen Adams; Toronto, University of Toronto Press 1983

Lightning Source UK Ltd.
Milton Keynes UK
UKHW010002210722
406167UK00001B/205

9 781487 598228